MARKETING FOR L___

Colin Gilligan
Professor of Marketing,
Sheffield Business School

Robin Lowe
Senior Lecturer in Marketing,
Sheffield Business School

Andrew Williamson
Solicitor and Managing Partner,
Walkers Solicitors

© *Colin Gilligan, Robin Lowe and Andrew Williamson* 1994

Published by
Central Law Publishing
A division of Central Law Training Ltd
Wrens Court
52/54 Victoria Road
Sutton Coldfield
Birmingham B72 1SX

ISBN 1 85811 029 7

All rights reserved. No part of this publication may be reproduced, stored in a retrieval system, or transmitted, in any form or by any means, electronic, mechanical, photocopying, recording or otherwise, without the prior permission of the publisher.

Printed in Great Britain by Ipswich Book Company Ltd.

The authors

Colin Gilligan is Professor of Marketing at Sheffield Business School. He is the author of books on advertising, business decision making, international marketing, marketing for the professions and strategic marketing management, and, most recently, strategic planning. Over the past ten years he has acted as a consultant to a wide variety of organisations, including numerous professional practices.

Robin Lowe is Senior Lecturer in Marketing and Head of the Small Business Research Unit at Sheffield Business School. He has had twenty five years experience in management and consultancy in both large and small organisations. He is the author of books on international marketing and, with Colin Gilligan, marketing for the professions.

Andrew Williamson is the Managing Partner of Walkers Solicitors, a medium sized firm in Bawtry and Retford. He is a member of the Institutes of Management and Quality and has undergone training as a Lead Assessor for quality management systems.

Dedication

This book is dedicated to the authors' wives – Rosie, Sylvia, and Pat, and children – Ben Gilligan, Jonathan and Catherine Lowe, and Laura and Emma Williamson, for their support; and to the lawyers whose marketing programme, it is hoped, will benefit from the book.

Contents

Preface vii

1 Introduction..1

2 So what is marketing? 11

3 Developing the client-centred firm: the first few steps......27

4 Client satisfaction and the role of marketing research......39

5 Environmental pressures and the parable of the boiled frog...........49

6 Planning for success (part one): assessing your planning skills 71

7 Planning for success (part two): developing the marketing plan 77

8 Using the marketing audit and the marketing effectiveness review to assess the true level of the firm's capability: revisiting your strengths and weaknesses 94

9 Developing the firm's marketing mix 108

10 Setting the standards of client care: the Blackpool rock phenomenon 130

11 Internal marketing, leadership and teamworking: fighting the Napoleonic complex..145

12 Implementing the plan and making things happen.........159

13 Scrivener and Proctor (Solicitors) 166

Index..171

Preface

This short book, which is based upon our experiences of working with a wide variety of professional practices over the past few years, is designed to provide lawyers with a clear understanding of the nature of marketing and of the ways in which it might possibly contribute to the effective management of their firms in the mid to late 1990s. In designing the book, we have deliberately concentrated upon producing short(ish) chapters that are capable not only of being easily digested in one sitting but which, by means of a series of questions and checklists, offer scope for being easily applied to individual firms of all types, sizes and specialisms.

In working your way through the book and its various checklists, you should not, however, focus just upon the individual questions that we pose, but should also spend time trying to identify the underlying picture that emerges. Is it the case, for example, that the partners really recognise the nature and significance of the changes taking place and have a strategy for coming to terms with them, or is it that there is a lack of any real strategy, with the partners being wedded to past and increasingly inappropriate approaches?

Having reached the end of the book, you should emerge with a far clearer idea not only of the nature and purpose of marketing, but also of the ways in which the firm can best make use of marketing techniques and, by means of a series of action plans, move ahead to make the most of the undoubted opportunities that exist. To help illustrate the applications of some of the concepts introduced, we have included at the end of the book a brief case study which we have called Scrivener and Proctor (Solicitors). Although this case is based very largely upon a firm for which we conducted a consultancy assignment, we have introduced elements from other firms and, in the finest traditions of the 1930's cinema industry, changed the names to protect the innocent (and, of course, the guilty).

The book follows what we hope will be seen as a logical framework, although perhaps the most important message must be, as one of our colleagues is fond of saying, TRY IT. "Try something," he suggests, "see how it works and then grow bolder. As Samuel Johnson said, it matters little which leg you put in the trousers first". Having read the book – and tried some of the ideas – let us know what happens; the second edition may well feature your own firm as a case study (your comments should be sent to Professor Colin Gilligan, Sheffield Business School, The Old Hall, Totley Hall Lane, Totley, Sheffield S17 4AB).

If you then feel sufficiently inspired to go further in your study of marketing, there are two other books which you might find useful:

Strategic Marketing Management: planning, implementation and control, by Professors Dick Wilson & Colin Gilligan (published by Butterworth Heinemann in 1992)

and *Strategic Marketing Planning* by Professors Colin Gilligan & Dick Wilson (to be published by Butterworth Heinemann in 1995)

Colin Gilligan
Robin Lowe
Andrew Williamson
December 1994

CHAPTER 1

The challenges facing law firms

> Having read this chapter, you should:
> - understand the nature and significance of the challenges facing law firms;
> - have a better understanding of the factors that contribute to good practice management; and
> - have gained an insight into the quality of the management within your firm.

The need for a more conscious, focused and proactive approach to the management of law firms has increased substantially over the last few years. Because of this, we begin this book not by plunging straight into a detailed discussion of the marketing process, but by taking a broader approach in which we highlight some of the challenges that lawyers are now having to face. Having done this, we move on to examine some of the characteristics of good and bad management practice. It is then against this background that in subsequent chapters we turn our attention to the question of marketing and how it might best contribute to the management of law firms as we move towards the 21st century.

THE CHALLENGES FACING SOLICITORS

As the first step along this road, refer to figure 1.1 and begin by identifying the six principal challenges which you believe your firm is likely to face and have to come to terms with in the short (that is the next twelve to eighteen months) and then in the longer term.

> **Figure 1.1 The short and long term challenges being faced by the firm**
>
> **The six principal challenges that the firm is likely to face in the short term and the long term are:**
>
> **Short term challenges**
>
> 1..
> 2..
> 3..
> 4..
> 5..
> 6..
>
> **Long term challenges**
>
> 1..
> 2..
> 3..
> 4..
> 5..
> 6..

Although the *particular* challenges faced will quite obviously vary – possibly significantly – from one firm to another, our work with almost fifty different firms over the past three years has identified a number of areas which practice managers and solicitors alike see as being of particular concern. These include:
- Legal aid franchising
- The adoption of the Law Society Practice Management Standards (before they possibly become compulsory)
- The advent of authorised Probate Practitioners
- The opening up of other areas of work to 'paralegals' and others
- A further contraction in the conveyancing market
- An extension of the limits for the small claims procedures in the County Court
- A tightening of the eligibility criteria for the granting of legal aid

- Continuing restrictions in legal aid funding
- The move towards mediation/conciliation in family proceedings
- The moves towards arbitration by non-lawyers in commercial cases
- The growing freedom for foreign lawyers to practise in this country
- A greater degree of accountability to clients
- A greater accountability to a seemingly ever more demanding Legal Aid Board
- Increased client choice and a greater willingness of clients to move from one firm to another
- Greater financial pressures
- A need for more attention to be paid to the firm's image
- A need to decide more clearly upon the focus of the firm and, in particular, which new and additional services to offer
- Whether some existing services should be pruned or dropped
- The need for many firms to develop more effective, and possibly more mature relationships with barristers' chambers and other experts
- An increased degree of intervention from government
- A need for more and better staff training and motivation
- An increase in the volume of paperwork
- Computerisation and data protection
- Increased client expectations and aggression, together with a greater willingness to complain
- The need for a more competitive philosophy
- Setting and meeting targets
- The need for better internal and external communication
- The better management of the relationship between the solicitors and the other members of the firm
- Issues of quality

Although this is not an exhaustive list and, as we comment above, the relative importance of each of the points is likely to vary greatly from one firm to another, it highlights the nature and breadth of the sorts of changes and challenges that are currently facing law firms and which the firm's management team need to come to terms with. From your viewpoint as a solicitor, the question that must be considered, of course, is how best can each of these challenges be managed. However, before trying to answer this, consider the questions in figure 1.2 and then ask yourself what message is beginning to emerge. Is it the case, for example, that the partners not only recognise the nature and significance of the current and emerging challenges and have begun to come to terms with them by means of a deliberate and strategic approach to the management of the firm, or is it that there is a general reluctance to change old habits and working practices?

> **Figure 1.2 Following on from the answers that you gave to the questions in figure 1.1:**
>
> 1 To what extent have these challenges been given *explicit* recognition in the firm?
>
> 2 What *specific* plans exist to deal with them?
>
> 3 Has the *responsibility* for dealing with these challenges been clearly allocated?

THE CHARACTERISTICS OF GOOD AND BAD MANAGEMENT

Over the past fifty years, a considerable amount has been written on the characteristics of good and bad management. One result of this is that a series of initially general but now increasingly specific guidelines exist. However, before looking at some of these, consider the question in figure 1.3:

> **Figure 1.3 The characteristics of good and bad management**
>
> **What do you consider to be the six principal characteristics of good and bad management?**
>
> | The characteristics of good management are: | The characteristics of bad management are: |
> |---|---|
> | 1.. | 1.. |
> | 2.. | 2.. |
> | 3.. | 3.. |
> | 4.. | 4.. |
> | 5.. | 5.. |
> | 6.. | 6.. |

The reality, of course, is that it is difficult (if not impossible) to identify the six or ten characteristics of good and bad management which will apply equally to every type and size of organisation. What we can do, however, is to identify the sorts of areas to which every organisation, be it a law firm or a multinational manufacturer of foodstuffs or cars, needs to give serious consideration. Included within these are:
- A statement of the organisation's mission and overall purpose
- The development of strong and positive values which are understood and adhered to by all staff and which the senior management are not prepared to compromise
- The development of clear and realistic objectives which, where possible, are agreed as the result of discussions amongst the staff so that there is a sense of shared ownership of the goals and strategy
- Strong and unambiguous patterns of communication which allow information to go upwards, downwards and sideways quickly without being distorted
- A sense of teamwork
- A clear allocation of responsibilities
- A sustained effort to motivate staff at all levels
- Systems for monitoring progress and feeding back the results, which then lead to corrective action being taken
- A climate which encourages rather than suppresses ideas
- A management philosophy which encourages a degree of independence amongst staff
- A management philosophy which encourages staff to get things done correctly on time
- Someone who takes responsibility for *driving* the strategy
- A recognition of staff needs (both personal and organisational)
- A willingness to experiment

AND, most importantly of all,
- An open and consistent management style, since one of the most widely accepted findings in management research is that one of the prime demotivators of staff is a lack of management consistency. Where the approach adopted fluctuates between autocratic, democratic and laissez-faire styles, seemingly depending upon how the wind is blowing, staff end up being confused and tend to focus upon a series of increasingly short term issues.

Taking each of these areas in turn, compare them firstly with the list of characteristics of good management that you developed for figure 1.3 and then, secondly, consider how well (or how badly) your firm scores; the framework for this appears in figure 1.4.

Figure 1.4 Scoring the quality of your firm's management

On a scale of 1-5 (1 being poor and 5 being very good), how does your firm score on each of the following dimensions of good management?

Score 1-5

1. The clarity of the mission and overall purpose .....
2. Strong and positive values .....
3. The clarity and appropriateness of the objectives .....
4. The effectiveness of communication patterns .....
5. The level of teamworking .....
6. The allocation of responsibilities .....
7. The levels of motivation .....
8. The use of monitoring systems .....
9. The encouragement of ideas .....
10. Staff independence .....
11. Getting things done correctly and on time .....
12. A strategy 'driver' .....
13. The recognition of staff needs .....
14. A willingness to experiment .....
15. The management style .....

Total .....

Scoring

With a total score of 29 or less, the firm is likely to lack direction and control with the result that motivation and morale almost inevitably will be low.

With a score of 30-50 there is scope for considerable improvement. With a score of 51-60, there is scope for some improvement, but you will probably have to work hard at this. There is certainly no room for complacency.

With a score of 61-75, you need to ask yourself just how honest you have been in your scoring process. If having done this, you still feel the score is justified, again you need to guard against complacency to ensure that your currently very high – and very rare – standards do not slip.

These sorts of ideas have also been brought together in the powerful and widely used 7-S model which was developed in the United States in the 1980s by the management consultants, McKinsey: this model has been given the title 'the 7-S framework'.

Figure 1.5 The McKinsey 7-S framework

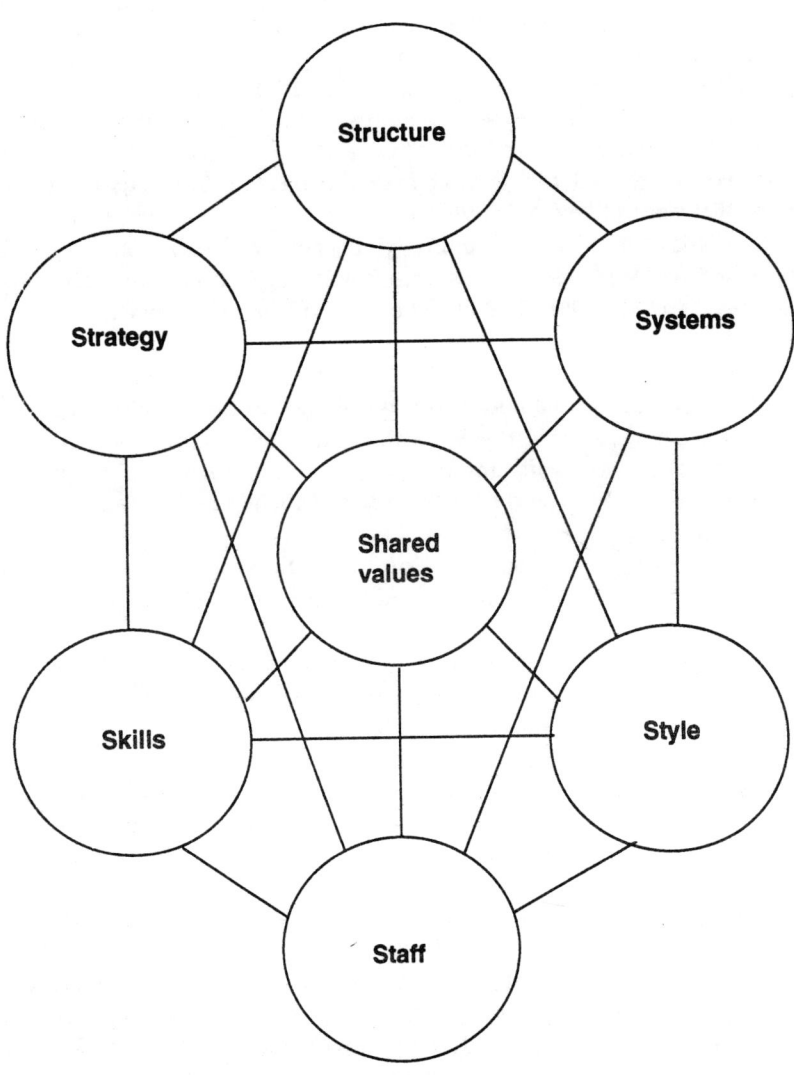

The importance of the first three elements – strategy, structure and systems – has long been recognised and are considered to be the *hardware* of successful management. The other four – style, staff, skills and shared values – are the *software*.

For much of the past fifty years, management thinking has been firmly based on the need for ensuring that the *hardware* elements exist. Thus, a successful organisation, it has been argued, builds on a *strategy* to achieve its goals, develops an appropriate organisational *structure* and then equips the organisation with the sorts of information, planning, control and reward *systems* needed to ensure that the job gets done. The starting point in this thinking is therefore that a strategy is needed before decisions on structure and systems are made.

The importance of the four *software* elements has been given substantially increased recognition over the past decade largely as the result of research work in what came to be labelled 'excellent' companies; these were organisations which achieved substantially better levels of performance and customer/client satisfaction than their competitors. The characteristics of these four *software* elements are:

Style: Employees share a broadly common way of thinking and behaving. In organisations such as Marks & Spencer and McDonald's, for example, all employees are taught to smile at customers and treat them in a particular and caring way.

Skills: Employees are fully trained in the sorts of skills that are needed to carry out the strategy.

Staff: The people recruited are capable, well-trained, and given the jobs which will best allow them to make use of their talents.

Shared values: The employees share the same values, understand where the organisation is going and what it stands for.

Given these comments, consider how your firm performs in relation to each of these dimensions; the framework for this appears in figure 1.6.

With regard to the software elements, arguably the most important single factor is the idea of shared values. There are several ways in which shared values can be developed within a firm, but especially by means of an open management style which encourages discussion,

---

Figure 1.6 Applying the McKinsey 7-S framework to your firm

1 Looking at each of the elements of the 7-S framework, how does your firm score? (1 = very poor, 5 = very good)

	Score 1-5
Strategy	....
Structure	....
Systems	....
Style	....
Skills	....
Staff	....
Shared values	....
Total	....

2 Where are the areas of greatest weakness?

3 What scope exists for improvement?

4 What are you planning to do about this?

---

communication, and a sense of common purpose amongst all staff, particularly within the management team. This will typically include solicitors, senior legal executives, office managers, senior accounts staff, and practice managers. Between you, you should therefore aim for a statement which brings together the *core values* of the firm (an example of this could be a fundamental commitment to quality and excellence which, irrespective of the circumstances, you are not willing to compromise), and a *vision* of the sort of firm that as a team you are trying to create. Having done this, there must then be a commitment to these values that is *consistently* reflected in the behaviour of the partners. Without this it is almost inevitable that the staff will all too quickly recognise that little more than lip service is being paid to these ideas with the result that their commitment to these values will quickly disappear.

SUMMARY

Within this chapter we have identified a number of the challenges that law firms are currently having to face and highlighted some of the principal characteristics of good and bad management. In the light of your answers to the questions that we have posed, consider the following:
1. What underlying picture of the firm emerges?
2. What do you feel are the principal causes of this picture, be it good or bad?
3. What sorts of answers do you feel that the staff within the firm might have given to the questions posed in figures 1.1, 1.2, 1.4 and 1.6? To what extent do these differ from your views? What are the reasons for and implications of this?

CHAPTER 2

So what is marketing?

> Having read this chapter, you should:
> - understand the marketing concept and how it can be applied within a law firm;
> - appreciate the significance of different stakeholder groups and the need to take their expectations into account;
> - understand the structure of the marketing process; and
> - appreciate the significance of the need for a distinct competitive stance.

Given the nature of our comments in Chapter 1, it is apparent that with law firms currently facing some of their biggest changes and challenges of the post-war period, the need for tighter, more professional and forward-looking management is now greater than ever before. In many cases this has meant a substantial rethink of how firms are run and how a variety of the managerial tools and techniques that previously were seen to be the prerogative of manufacturers in the private sector – and hence of little real relevance to solicitors – might now possibly contribute to the better and more effective management of their firms. Prominent amongst these is the whole area of marketing. In many cases, however, there appears still to be a fundamental misunderstanding amongst solicitors of precisely what marketing involves and how it might most realistically contribute either to the effective day-to-day management of the firm, or indeed to its longer term development.

In this chapter we concentrate on overcoming some of the more common preconceptions and misconceptions that we have come across in our discussions with lawyers and move towards developing a framework which should go some way towards establishing a stronger – and far more effective – marketing and client-centred orientation within the firm.

WHAT MARKETING IS AND WHAT MARKETING IS NOT

As a starting point, consider the four statements in figure 2.1 to see which corresponds most closely with your view of marketing.

Figure 2.1 Marketing is.......

1 ....the same as advertising
2 ....something which is used solely by manufacturing organisations and therefore of little or no real relevance to lawyers
3 ....manipulative and a disguised approach to a hard sell
4 ....an approach to management which applies to all types of organisation, since it puts the customer (in the case of law firms this is, of course, the client) at the very centre of the operation and directs resources in such a way that the customer achieves a high level of satisfaction in a cost effective manner.

Those of you who answered 'yes' to any, or indeed all, of the first three should go to the bottom of the class. Those who agreed with number four get top marks.

So what then is wrong with the first three statements? In the case of the first of these, we can illustrate its limitations by focusing upon examples of large organisations whose activities you will undoubtedly be familiar with and which have developed a strong reputation for consistently effective marketing and high levels of customer satisfaction. If we ask members of the public to identify three or four examples of the sorts of organisations which they consider to be good at marketing, the same names almost invariably crop up. Prominent amongst these are Coca Cola, McDonald's, Marks and Spencer, and Body Shop. In the case of Coca Cola and McDonald's, both companies concentrate upon using substantial amounts of advertising to communicate clear and simple messages (Things go better with Coke and There's nothing quite like a McDonald's) which are understood and meaningful to customers across the world. They market consistently reliable products and provide levels of service which rarely disappoint. Marks and Spencer, by contrast, has achieved a similarly strong position with little or no advertising, whilst Body Shop is successful despite spending very little on advertising, packaging or indeed store layout.

Marketing and advertising are not, therefore, one and the same thing. Rather, advertising is just one of the marketing tools available.

On a much smaller scale, think about your favourite restaurant. Although at first sight it might appear that it does not need marketing to make it successful, look more closely on your next visit. Almost inevitably it will have built a clear reputation as, for example, the best Italian, Indian or Chinese restaurant in town. The appearance and decoration will project a clear image, the staff will be friendly and the food and drinks will have been selected to meet the demands and expectations of the customers who will be made to feel comfortable in these surroundings. To create a successful restaurant, every aspect will have been planned well in advance, reflecting the owners' and manager's beliefs about what the customers they wish to attract will want. However, their task does not end there as they will constantly be trying to improve things and make sure that every aspect of the restaurant is just right. So marketing can but does not need to depend on advertising, and is capable of making just as important a contribution to the success of small as well as large organisations.

The third common misconception is that marketing is almost invariably manipulative and is quite simply hard selling in disguise; timeshare holiday companies are a notorious example of this. In the long term, however, customer satisfaction cannot be built on manipulation or on false promises. Customers may fall victim to it the first time, but only rarely on a second occasion. In the case of timeshare, most members of the public, and not just those who have fallen foul of the timeshare touts, are now only too aware of the exaggerated offers that they typically make and are suspicious of almost *any* offer that is made, regardless of how attractive it appears. The unfortunate result of this has, of course, been that the reputable companies in the industry (and yes, they do exist) which offer a worthwhile product have been affected as well. Because of this, the opportunity for the market to be developed to its full potential has been lost – probably for ever – not necessarily because of any failure of the product or service offered, but because of the unacceptably high-pressure selling techniques that have been used.

Given these examples, we should be in a far clearer position to identify what marketing in its truest sense means and what it involves. Although it is difficult to list *all* of the activities that are typically covered by marketing, the most important can be identified as:
(i) monitoring the external environment (what is happening outside the organisation and over which it has no control) with a view to identifying opportunities and threats;

(ii) contributing to the discussion about the nature and direction that the organisation should pursue and the competitive stance that should be adopted;
(iii) determining the range of products or services that should be offered;
(iv) influencing the levels of customer/client satisfaction that are to be aimed for;
(v) deciding upon the image that is to be projected;
(vi) managing the elements of the marketing mix on a day-to-day basis (the make-up of the mix is discussed at a later stage in the chapter); and
(vii) developing and implementing a system of feedback and control that is capable of providing a clear picture of just how well the organisation is performing.

It follows from this that the essence of good marketing in all organisations, including law firms, involves both a strong *external* and a clear *internal* orientation. *External* in that we are concerned with building a clear picture of what is happening currently and what is likely to happen in the future outside the organisation so that we might identify and capitalise upon any opportunities that exist and take action to avoid or minimise the impact of any threats, and *internal* in terms of making sure that what we offer and intend doing is appropriate, feasible and that the staff understand and are fully committed to this.

DEFINITIONS OF MARKETING

It should be apparent from what has been said so far that marketing is a much more complex activity than simply selling or advertising the product or service that the organisation, be it Marks and Spencer or a solicitor's practice, has decided to provide, something which is reflected in the numerous definitions of marketing that exist; figure 2.2 shows just a small selection of these.

Whilst you might feel that some changes in the definition are needed to reflect the specifics of your own firm's situation, the core elements of *analysis, anticipation* and *meeting the requirements of clients* are fundamental. It is for this reason that, for us, the most meaningful definition of marketing is:

> Marketing is all about developing a really meaningful competitive advantage, and then exploiting it to the full.

So what is marketing?

> **Figure 2.2 Definitions of marketing**
>
> - Marketing is the management process for identifying, anticipating and satisfying customers' requirements profitably. (Source: Chartered Institute of Marketing)
> - Marketing is the central dimension of any business. It is the whole business seen from the point of view of its final result, that is from the customers' point of view. (Source: Peter Drucker)
> - Marketing is all about customer satisfaction and moving heaven and earth to achieve this more effectively than other organisations. (Anon)
> - The marketing concept represents an 'outside-in' view of the organisation, in that a deliberate attempt is made to look at the organisation and its products/services from the viewpoint of the customer. In doing this, a far greater emphasis is placed upon meeting customers' needs, emphasising the product's benefits, achieving higher levels of internal coordination, and generally achieving a far better match between what the customers want and what the organisation provides. (Source: Colin Gilligan and Robin Lowe)

In making this comment, we have several thoughts in mind. Perhaps the most obvious is that if your firm does not have a clearly developed (and meaningful) competitive advantage or strong selling proposition, there is no reason why a prospective client should come to you rather than go to a competitor. However, having developed a competitive advantage, you need then to exploit it to the full.

SO WHAT IS A COMPETITIVE ADVANTAGE? ESTABLISHING THE COMPETITIVE STANCE

At its most basic, a competitive advantage is anything that you are capable of doing more effectively than another firm. However, in many cases the sorts of things that organisations view as a competitive advantage are perceived by clients to be of little real significance. In thinking about competitive advantage, you should therefore focus upon the possible bases for differentiating your firm from its competitors in a way that clients will see to be of value to them. All too often, however, firms of solicitors end up doing broadly the same thing and projecting an image that is essentially the same as every firm in the locality.

To help in the process of developing a competitive advantage and a distinct (and distinctive) competitive stance, figure 2.3 provides a useful starting point. The thinking behind the diagram is straightforward and reflects the idea that there are in essence only three possible generic competitive strategies: a cost/price based strategy; market focusing or niching; and a differentiated approach.

Figure 2.3 The bases of competition

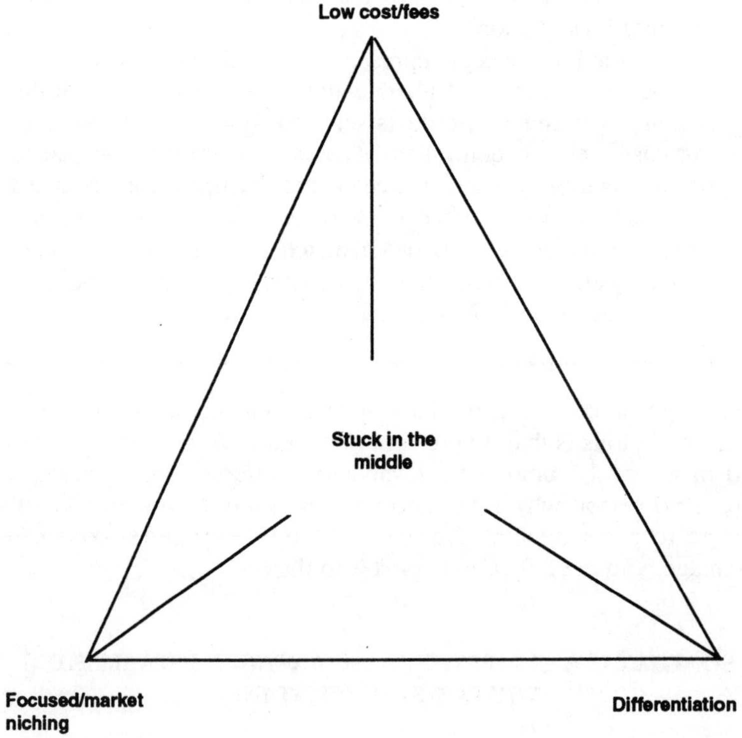

Low cost/fees

Stuck in the middle

Focused/market niching **Differentiation**

The first of these, a cost/price based strategy, is exactly what the words suggest and reflects four beliefs:
1. that low fees are the most important single influence upon the client's choice of solicitor;
2. that the low price message can be communicated to the market;
3. that a price-based strategy is sustainable; and
4. that it will prove profitable.

By contrast, a market nicher focuses upon what are often highly specific areas of client need and then concentrates upon building a reputation as one of the few specialists in this area; an example of this would be as a specialist in intellectual property.

The third competitive strategy – differentiation – is based on the idea that clients are not necessarily motivated primarily by cost and do not have a highly specific need. Instead, they are attracted by a package of factors such as the firm's breadth and depth of experience, its size, location, general reputation, and so on. It is then the unique combination of these that enables the firm to achieve a differentiated position.

In many cases, however, the choice of strategy is either inappropriate for the market or it is pursued with insufficient clarity (in other words, the market fails to understand the message and does not perceive the practice in the way intended). The result is a confused market position in which the firm ends up stuck in the middle with no obvious distinguishing characteristics. In these circumstances, there is no *real* reason why a prospective client should choose one firm rather than another. The reality, of course, is that many firms of solicitors, particularly in the provinces, find themselves in this stuck in the middle position. As generalists, they have few opportunities to differentiate themselves from their competitors in the same building, street or town, other than by means of the least attractive form of competition – low fees.

Recognising this and the importance of a clear and sustainable competitive stance, consider the following questions:
1 What is the primary element of your competitive strategy currently? (Where do you appear in figure 2.3?)
2 How are your competitors competing?
3 What image do you have currently?
4 What areas of specialism exist within the firm?
5 What scope do they offer as a basis for a more proactive strategy?
6 What areas of market need exist? In what ways might they be reflected in a more obvious competitive strategy?

THE SIGNIFICANCE OF STAKEHOLDERS

Although in a legal practice, the main strand of any definition of marketing that we use might be translated into *meeting clients' needs*, there is a strong case for arguing that this is too simplistic, since if the practice is to be successful, account needs to be taken not just of clients' needs but also those of a variety of other stakeholders (a stakeholder is any individual or group which has an interest in how the firm operates); these are illustrated in figure 2.4.

Figure 2.4 The firm's stakeholders

Each stakeholder approaches an organisation with certain expectations and it is the extent to which these expectations are satisfied that is the true measure of organisational effectiveness. Recognising this, turn to figure 2.5 and identify in as much detail as possible the nature of each of your stakeholder's expectations and the scope for any conflict that exists between the different types of stakeholder.

So what is marketing?

Figure 2.5 Stakeholders' expectations of our firm

Clients..

Those associated with the client...

Suppliers..

The Legal Aid Board..

Partners and staff..

Introducers of business..

The courts..

The Law Society..

Society at large..

Scope for conflict exists between these expectations in the following areas:

- ....
- ....
- ....
- ....

Overall, how well do you feel that you manage any conflict that exists?..
....

What else might you do?..
....

THE TWO LEVELS OF MARKETING

If marketing is to make a significant contribution to a law firm, it needs to operate at two levels. At its most fundamental it represents the development of a clear and appropriate competitive stance and the pursuit of an underlying philosophy of client satisfaction which should guide everything that the solicitors and staff do. On a day-to-day level, it is concerned with issues such as the specifics of the service that is offered, the image that is projected, and how and where the service is

to be presented. The essence of marketing is therefore to get everyone to pull together and work towards the common goal of customer/client satisfaction. If this is done, and done effectively, the benefits can be considerable and include:
- higher levels of client satisfaction;
- a far greater likelihood of identifying market opportunities in their early stages;
- a higher level of awareness of those factors that will ultimately prove to be a threat;
- a better sense of direction and co-ordination;
- a greater opportunity for staff to take more responsibility without loss of control; and
- higher levels of staff motivation as a result of their greater understanding, involvement, responsibility and commitment.

THE MARKETING PROCESS

In the light of our comments so far, we can identify the principal strands of a marketing programme as being concerned with the development of a clear understanding of three distinct elements:
1 The pressures of the environment (and hence the nature of any opportunities and threats that exist currently and which are likely to emerge in the future).
2 The demands, needs or expectations of clients and how these are likely to change.
3 What the firm is *really* capable of delivering.

It follows from this that the marketing process consists of four stages:
1 Analysis
2 Planning
3 Evaluation and implementation
4 Feedback and control

These are illustrated in figure 2.6 and expanded upon in figure 2.7.

Stage One: Market analysis

The first of these four stages involves developing a clear understanding of the variety of factors outside the firm which for the most part cannot be controlled but which determine how the firm operates and which are capable of having a very real influence upon performance. Included within this is the general environment, the changing needs of clients and other stakeholders, and the behaviour of competitors.

Figure 2.6 The marketing process

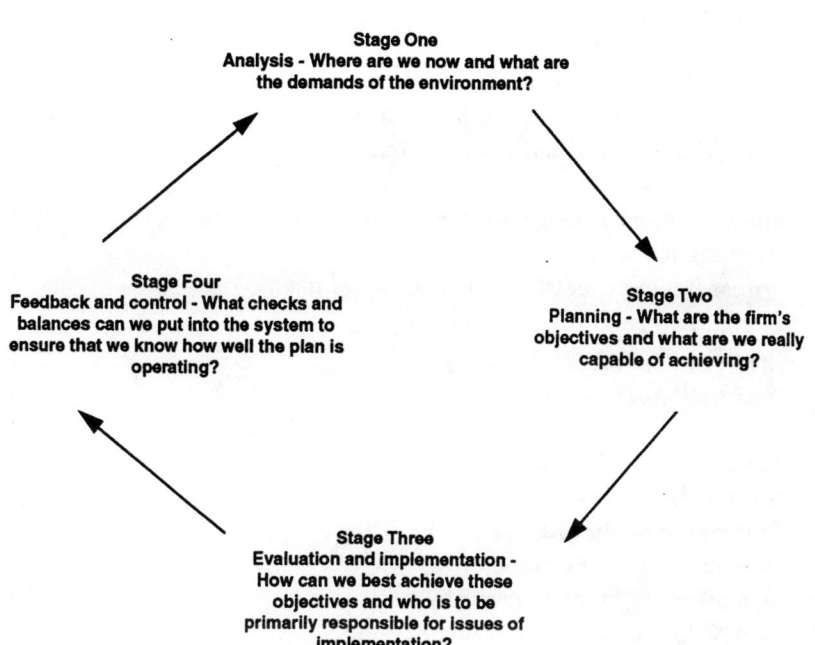

> **Figure 2.7 The four stages of the marketing process**
>
> **Stage One: Analysis (Where are we now?)**
> Analysing and understanding:
> - the environment;
> - the clients' and other stakeholders' needs and expectations;
> - the competition (what other firms are doing and what we can learn from them and improve upon).
>
> **Stage Two: Planning (Where do we want to go?)**
> Planning for action by:
> - researching clients' current and future needs;
> - setting objectives and standards;
> - evaluating the firm's capabilities;
> - planning for change.
>
> **Stage Three: Evaluation and implementation (How might we get there?)**
> Implementing the plan by:
> - managing the marketing mix;
> - marketing the plan internally;
> - developing stakeholder relationships;
>
> **Stage Four: Feedback and control (How can we check how well the plan is operating?)**
> Controlling the plan by:
> - developing checks and balances
> - monitoring progress
> - taking corrective action

Stage Two: Marketing planning

Against the background of what emerges from the market analysis, the emphasis needs then to shift to planning and, in particular, to the identification of the goals, objectives and standards which the firm will pursue. In doing this, detailed consideration needs to be given to an assessment of the firm's true capabilities, since these determine how likely it is that objectives will be met and whether any gaps exist between the firm's aspirations, objectives and its capabilities (in other words, what you are *really* capable of delivering). This information can then be brought together in the form of a marketing plan which will be the blueprint for development.

Stage Three: Evaluating and implementing the plan

Following this, the focus turns to the question of how to implement the plan. It has long been recognised that the implementation stage is typically the most difficult part of the marketing planning process, since it is only too easy to lose sight of the objectives, to be blown off course by unforseen events, and to become preoccupied with day-to-day pressures with the result that longer term issues are ignored. A key element of marketing is therefore concerned with how best to manage the resources that are available in as effective a manner as possible and ensure that the objectives that have been set are achieved. Because the largest and most costly resource in law firms is that of the staff, much of the implementation phase is, of necessity, concerned with mobilising the staff and other stakeholders, including those who supply the firm with services and products, by making sure that they fully understand what is expected of them and that they then contribute in the most appropriate way.

But as well as staff, implementation is integrally tied up with how well the marketing mix is managed. Although we discuss the marketing mix in detail in Chapter 9, there are several comments that can usefully be made at this stage. The marketing mix, which consists of the seven elements illustrated in figures 2.8 and 2.9, and which is sometimes referred to as the 7Ps, represents the marketing man or woman's tool kit and is made up of the various elements that, despite the strict guidelines and controls that exist within law firms, can be *managed* in order to shape the profile of the firm that is presented to the world. As such, the appropriateness of the mix (that is, the match between the mix and the demands of the environment) has a direct influence upon the firm's performance.

Stage Four: Feedback and control

Having implemented the marketing plan, attention needs then to be paid to measuring the performance levels that are being achieved with a view to identifying where scope exists for modification and

Figure 2.8 The seven elements of the marketing mix

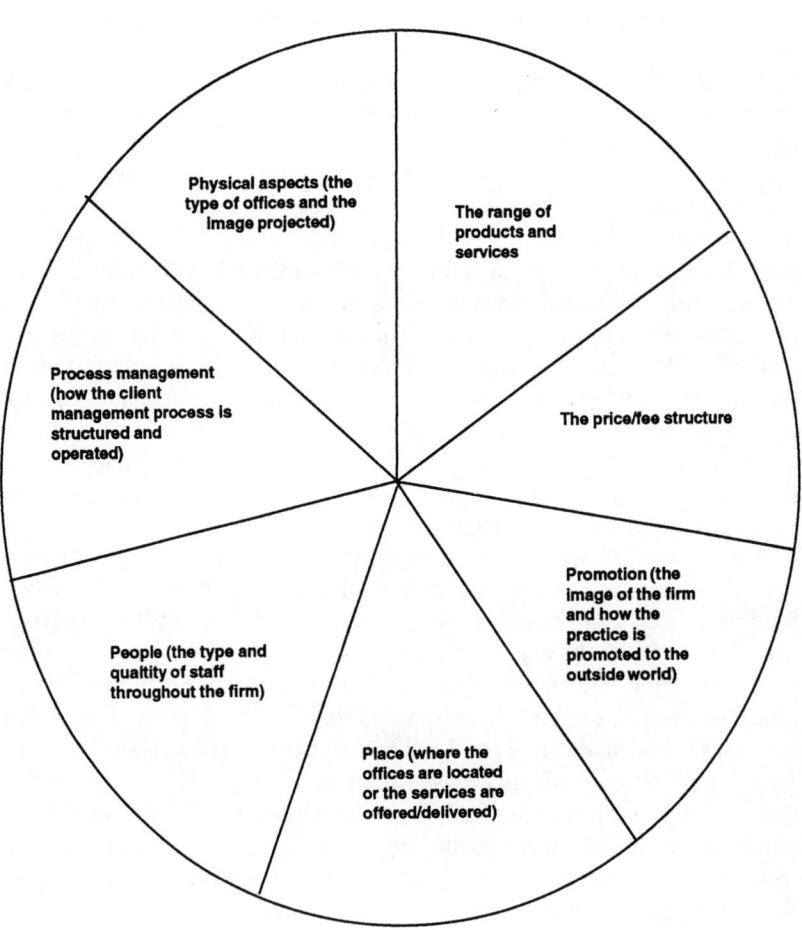

So what is marketing? 25

Figure 2.9 The marketing mix and the legal environment

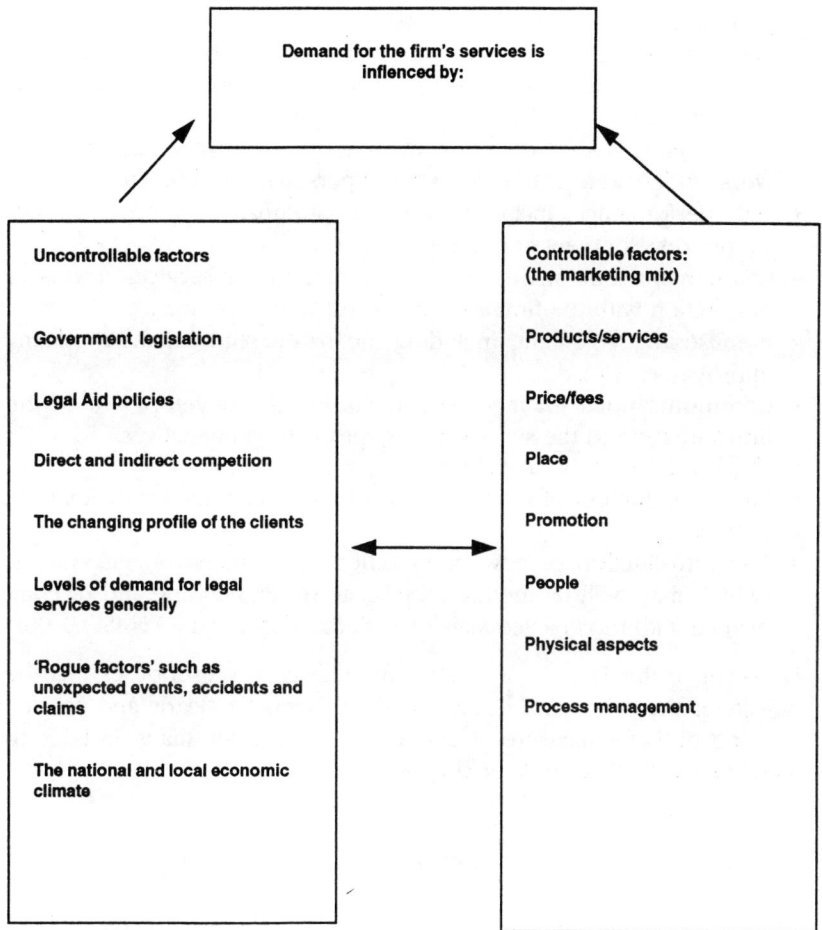

improvement. There is, therefore, a need to monitor performance under a variety of headings. These might include:
- Financial performance, including income, expenditure and profitability.
- Relative competitive performance (how well or badly has the firm performed in relation to those firms that are seen to be direct competitors?).
- Each solicitor's level of commitment and performance, including the work undertaken, external posts and personal development.
- Staff performance, including turnover, attitudes, absenteeism, motivation, development and training.
- Client management, including the demand for services, levels of satisfaction with the firm and clients lost to competitors.
- Premises management, including the nature and suitability of any improvements made.
- Communications management, including the development of the firm's image and the success of any promotional initiatives.
- The levels and type of publicity.
- The development of new services such as estate agency or financial services.
- The introduction of new or modified client management systems (which may well be required for Legal Aid Franchising and/or compliance with the Practice Management Standards or BS EN ISO 9000).

However, if this is to be a meaningful activity, it presupposes that the objectives that were set in stage two have been set clearly and provide a sound basis for measure or comparison over time; this is an issue to which we will return in later chapters.

SUMMARY

Within this chapter we have focused upon the nature of marketing and the marketing process as well as the ways in which marketing is capable of being applied within law firms. Although a marketing programme needs to reflect, or at least take account of the expectations of various stakeholder groups, the primary focus is that of how best to develop a truly client-oriented firm. It is this issue which is developed in the next chapter.

CHAPTER 3

Developing the client-centred firm: the first few steps

> Having read this chapter, you should:
> - understand the dimensions of a client-centred firm;
> - appreciate the significance of the differences between features and benefits;
> - have a clearer insight to the benefits that your firm offers currently and is capable of offering in the future; and
> - understand in greater detail what it is that your clients want from the firm.

In order to develop a marketing-oriented and truly client-centred firm, there is an obvious need to understand in detail your market for legal services and, in particular, the sorts of factors that are likely to lead to higher levels of client satisfaction. Without this information, any marketing effort will be unfocused and, at best, of only limited value. So what is it that contributes to client satisfaction? Although most solicitors would argue that they have a clear idea of this, it is only the clients themselves who are *really* able to answer the question. There are, however, lessons that can be learned from the traditional home of marketing – the consumer goods sector – that help to provide a degree of insight into how we might best go about this.

Whenever we begin a consultancy assignment, we pose a deceptively simple question: what *benefits* are your customers really looking for? The significance of this is that only rarely, if ever, do people buy a product or service for its own sake. Instead, they buy it for the benefits that it provides. Perhaps the most commonly cited example of this is the purchase of a drill which, as the American management guru Theodeore Levitt pointed out in the 1950s, is bought not for its physical qualities but in order to provide holes. It follows from this that a manufacturer of twist drills will eventually go out of business if a laser can do the job twice as accurately, twice as fast and at half the cost.

By the same token, cars such as Porsche, Mercedes, BMW and Jaguar, which typically litter city car parks, whether we like to admit it or not, are bought as much for their status, image and prestige as anything else. We then justify the purchase by highlighting features such as the build quality, the glacier-like depreciation, the pre and after-sales services, reliability, and so on. By the same token, research in the expensive boxed chocolates market reveals that the buying motives are only rarely concerned with taste, but are instead more commonly to do with the perceived value of the product as a gift. In the case of the beer market, the primary buying motives amongst the 18-22 year olds have consistently been shown to be concerned not with the beer's taste or strength, but with the images associated with the brand and peer group pressure.

Recognition of this highlights the need for a clear and detailed understanding of the distinctions that exist between features and benefits, since it is this understanding which underpins any attempt to develop a truly client-centred firm. It is, for example, only too easy to talk about the sorts of things that solicitors do (the features) rather than what clients get from them (the benefits). The way in which this is typically manifested is in terms of how a solicitor solves a client's problem. The application of legal skills is the *feature*. However, looking at it from the clients' point of view, they go to a solicitor with a problem wanting it to be solved. The extent to which this is achieved is influenced only partly by the legal skills used. The other part of the solution consists of a series of non-legal elements that are normally referred to as client care (this typically includes the reception and other support staff and the general client management process). If these non-legal elements fail to work effectively, the client may well go away having been provided with a solution to the problem but feeling unhappy, unconvinced by the legal process and generally dissatisfied. This creates the paradoxical situation where you might well have used the highest possible level of legal skills to obtain an excellent result, yet the client may be unaware of this, having judged your performance on the tangible non-legal elements of the service.

COMING TO TERMS WITH THE BENEFITS

In order to understand more fully the sorts of benefits that the firm offers currently, you need to begin by looking at features from the viewpoint of the client. There are several ways of doing this, although perhaps the most useful is by focusing in turn upon each of the seven principal elements of the marketing mix. Although the detail of the mix is discussed at a later stage in Chapter 9, we identified its components in Chapter 2 (see pages 24 and 25) and can illustrate the features/benefit distinction here by focusing upon just one of these dimensions, that of the product or service.

The cornerstone of any marketing programme is the nature of the product or service offered, since virtually all other marketing elements and decisions are directly influenced by what we offer. In the case of law firms, the product/service is the collection of benefits that the client desires. At the core of this 'product' are the legal services in which the traditional issues of excellence, quality and expertise are paramount; examples of those that are typically offered appear in figure 3.1.

Figure 3.1: The core legal services

- probate and wills
- matrimonial
- conveyancing
- trusts and tax planning
- company and commercial work
- personal injury claims
- general litigation
- crime
- housing
- consumer problems

It is worth pausing for a moment to look in slightly more detail at the composition of the core legal services. Up to now, we have assumed that they only mean the application of strictly legal skills possessed uniquely by solicitors. Consider, however, house conveyancing which has traditionally been the staple diet of the average firm until the present recession. Whilst some knowledge of the law is essential, most house transactions are typically characterised by proficiency in administrative skills and coordinating a related chain of transactions. If public libraries had a computer link to the Land Registry so that the process could be achieved by pressing a button or two, solicitors would inevitably suffer the same fate as the twist-drill manufacturer faced with competition from lasers. Think carefully, therefore, about each of your services and distinguish the components of it that must be done by qualified lawyers from other areas. Apart from identifying those services that are most at risk from non-lawyer competitors, you will see what work can be delegated internally and which may save costs.

Surrounding these core legal services are the various non-legal support services, including the appointments system, the receptionists, the waiting area, the manner of the interview itself and how contact is maintained between the solicitor and client (included within this is the nature of the correspondence); these are illustrated in figure 3.2.

Although the question of what benefits the firm offers currently and what it is capable of developing is considered in far greater detail in Chapter 9, a useful first step at this stage is to begin by thinking about the nature and significance of the benefits that clients get from the services you offer. In doing this, Herzberg's two-factor theory of motivation can be of some help. The theory distinguishes between *satisfiers* (factors that create satisfaction) and *dissatisfiers* (factors that create dissatisfaction). In the case of a car, for example, the absence of a warranty would be a dissatisfier. The existence of a warranty, however, is not a satisfier in itself since it is not one of the principal reasons for buying the car; as we commented at an earlier stage, these are more likely to be the car's looks, its performance and the status that the driver feels that it confers.

There are several implications of this theory for the marketing of law firms, the two most significant of which are, first, that the seller (that is, the solicitor and the firm) needs to be fully aware of the dissatisfiers which, while they will not by themselves sell the product, can easily 'unsell' it (for example, clients soon tire of being routinely kept waiting for appointments, especially when the appointment has been made well in advance). The second implication, which follows logically from this, is that solicitors and support staff need to understand in detail the various satisfiers and then concentrate not just upon supplying them, but also giving emphasis to them so that clients are fully aware of them. For example, some firms give their clients a document folder at end of a conveyancing transaction. If this is more than the client was expecting, particular satisfaction will be generated.

It should be apparent from this that achieving a truly client-centred firm is a potentially difficult task and, for most firms, is likely to involve significant changes in operating practice and culture. Recognising this, consider the following questions and then move on to the checklist that appears in figure 3.3.

- What are the principal satisfiers and dissatisfiers within the firm?
- What are we doing/can we do to increase the satisfiers and reduce or abolish completely the dissatisfiers?
- What are the obstacles to making the sorts of changes needed in order to achieve a client-centred firm, how significant are they, and how might we overcome them?

Figure 3.2: The product/service and the surrounding support mechanisms

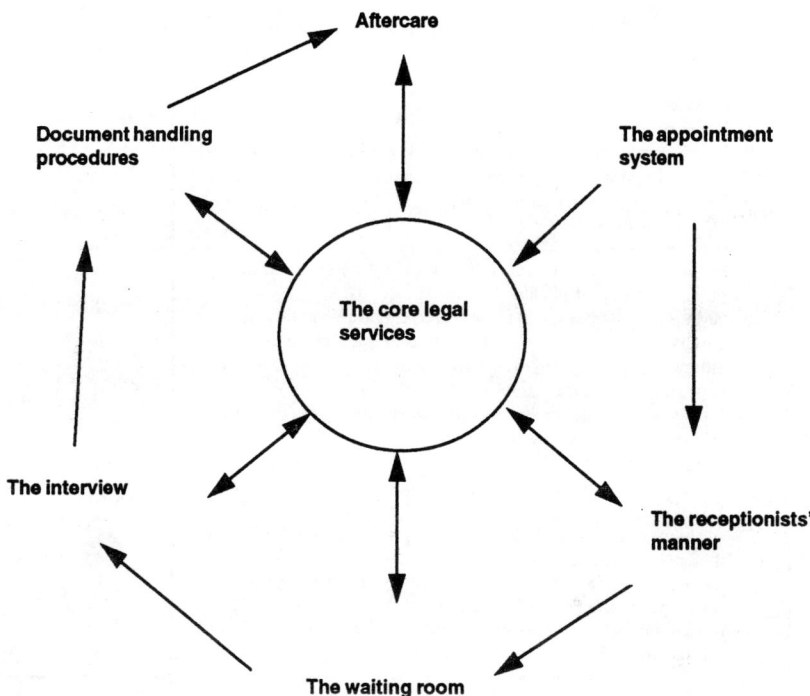

Figure 3.3 How serious are we about client satisfaction?

Marks out of ten
1 = Very poor performance;
5 = Average performance but with possibly considerable scope for improvement;
10 = Excellent performance.

How good are we at:
1. Measuring levels of client satisfaction?
2. Using measures of client satisfaction to change the firm's policies and operating procedures?
3. Using client satisfaction measures to
   (a) evaluate staff
   (b) reward staff?
4. Ensuring that *all* staff have a clear understanding of our policy on client care and quality?
5. Setting measurable goals for levels of client care and quality?
6. Discussing with staff the clients' needs and expectations?
7. Taking formal note of what staff say about clients' needs and expectations and the extent to which they are being met?
8. Setting a good example as solicitors of the levels of service and quality that we *say* are important?
9. Providing opportunities for staff to work together to overcome obstacles in order to achieve high(er) levels of quality and service?
10. Evaluating how other firms operate and the standards that they are achieving?
11. Evaluating what organisations outside the legal profession do with a view to learning from them?
12. Implementing a clearly stated and realistic policy on client service and quality?

Total score (out of 120)

The Scoring Process
Each lawyer within the firm should work through the twelve questions in order to arrive at a score. The scores are then aggregated and averaged. The overall measures of commitment to client service and satisfaction can then be assessed against the following scale:
With a score of 59 or less, questions can be asked about the firm's commitment to client care. Fundamental changes are needed, both in the firm's philosophy and organisational structure.
With a score of between 60-79, there is again scope for improvement.
With a score of between 80-99, scope for improvement still exists, although this is likely to be in terms of a series of small changes and modifications rather than anything more fundamental.
With a score of 100 or more, care needs to be taken that solicitors and staff maintain the standards being achieved and that complacency does not creep in.

Adapted from Piercy, N (1991), *Market-led Strategic Change*, page 55, Thursons.

BUT ARE THE APPARENT BENEFITS REALLY BENEFITS?

Perhaps the easiest and most useful way of identifying and assessing the sorts of benefits that clients might get from a service is to apply the 'which means that' and the 'so what?' tests; these are illustrated in figures 3.4 and 3.5. Most firms only offer appointments throughout the day, so for a firm considering offering longer opening hours, the implication of the 'which means that' test is that clients would not be tied to office hours. The potential benefits for a person who is not free during the course of the day are therefore obvious. However, for a person who can only attend the office in the daytime the 'so what?' test highlights that the change is of no real or direct value (there may, of course, be the indirect benefit that because appointments are being spread throughout a longer day, an appointment should be easier to make).

Given this, and recognising that the benefits to clients are not always as obvious or as significant as might have been hoped or expected at first sight, figure 3.5 can be used to identify – and, more importantly, assess – the *real* benefits of any features that you offer currently or are thinking of developing.

SO WHAT DO CLIENTS REALLY WANT FROM THEIR SOLICITORS?

Before looking at the question of client wants, it is worthwhile taking a moment to consider the real underlying needs of the client. In most cases, needs and wants are one and the same thing, although there are instances where great care must be taken to diagnose the client's own perception of the situation. For instance, in matrimonial cases some clients will come in and ask for a divorce because that is all that they have heard of from friends or the media. In some cases, however, it may not be in their best interests to have a divorce; an obvious example would be where there are pension rights that would be lost upon divorce. The client is probably better advised to pursue judicial separation, particularly (as often is the case) where there are no immediate plans to remarry. The question of divorce can always then be looked into at a later date.

The importance to clients of this diagnostic phase is recognised by the surveys which are regularly reported in the legal press. Invariably, technical competence features as one of the most important criteria for selection of a lawyer. However, clients want lawyers who not only possess that basic technical competence, but also the ability to identify the root cause of a problem, even if the advice that they are given proves to be unpalatable.

Figure 3.4 The features – benefit link

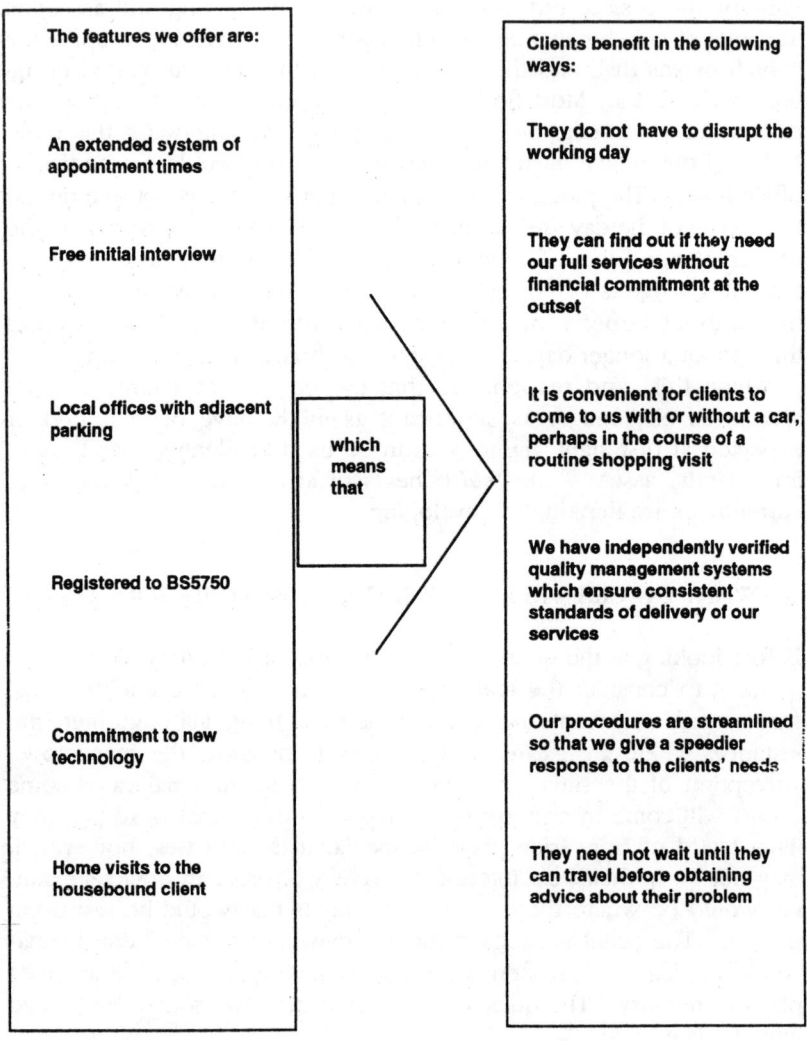

Figure 3.5: The features, benefits and 'so what?' link

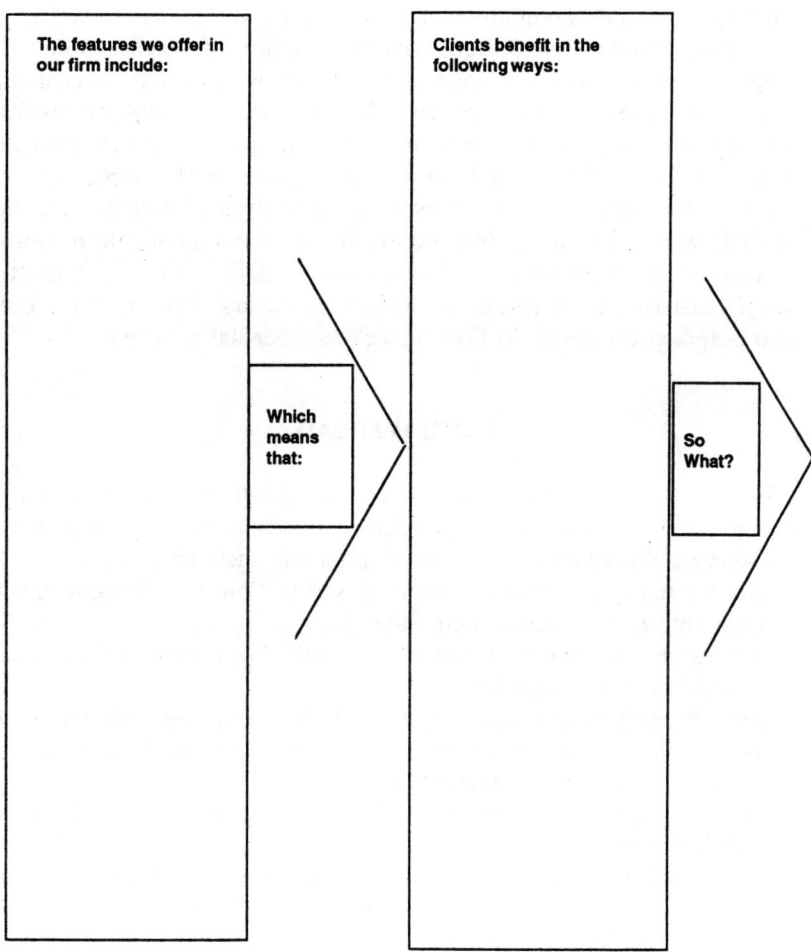

Those same surveys, however, also highlight the importance of communication skills and the need to keep clients updated. According to the Solicitors Complaints Bureau, at least 80% of all complaints can be attributed to poor communication, something which has now been recognised by the Law Society with the creation of Practice Rule 15, requiring firms to communicate more frequently and more effectively with their clients. This is an issue that has particular implications for the support staff, as they will probably have more personal contact with each client of the firm, both on the telephone and in person, than the admitted staff. By way of example, it is always worth bearing in mind how much business is done on the telephone (a significant proportion of total fees are earned in telephone calls) so the receptionist/telephonist can have enormous influence not just upon existing but also potential clients of the firm, as well as other stakeholders.

MOVING AHEAD

Given the nature of these comments, the question of how the truly client-centred firm might be developed needs to be approached by considering the answer to a series of questions, including:
- Do we *really* know what levels of satisfaction and dissatisfaction exist amongst our clients currently?
- Where clients are dissatisfied, do we *really* know how deep and/or justified this dissatisfaction is?
- Are we *really* aware of the causes of client irritation with the firm and are there any common strands between any causes for complaint/dissatisfaction that clients might have?
- Do we *really* understand what leads to high(er) levels of client satisfaction?
- Would we *really* be willing to make possibly radical changes in how we operate in order to achieve higher levels of client satisfaction?
- Have we *really* done enough to train our staff or do we rely upon common-sense and learning from the long-established members of the firm?
- How much money would we *really* be willing to invest in training and facilities in order to achieve higher levels of client satisfaction?

In the light of your answers to the various questions that we have posed in this chapter and the score that has emerged from the checklist in figure 3.3, you should have some understanding of the nature of the firm's orientation and the extent to which it is really client-centred. Our experience has shown that firms can be viewed very broadly in

Developing the client-centred firm: the first few steps 37

Figure 3.6 The solicitor centred/client centred continuum

The solicitor centred practice is characterised by a belief that:

- legal practice has not really changed since the 1920s and change is something that should be resisted
- clients are fundamentally a nuisance
- office hours should be based on what is most convenient to the partners
- the reception staff are there to keep clients away from the solicitors as much as possible
- the firm's office is regarded as a cost, which must be kept to a minimum, rather than an investment
- solicitors always know best

The **client** centred firm is characterised by:

- a clear understaning of how clients' needs and the benefits they are seeking
- a willingness to adapt the firm and its operating approaches to meet these needs fully
- clients keep the firm in existence
- an understanding of how rival firms operate and what can be learned from them
- a willingness to experiment
- a listening approach
- the development of new and client relevant services
- an appointments system which is designed to suit clients' needs
- a willingness to invest in better facilities including the waiting room
- a well thought out programme of training for fee earners and support staff

terms of a continuum ranging from at the one end the inward looking and old-fashioned firm in which clients know their place and dare not move from this, through to the highly client-centred firm at the other; this is illustrated in figure 3.6.

In most cases, of course, firms do not appear at one extreme or the other but are instead located at some point along the continuum. In identifying where on this you are, you should therefore focus not so much upon the specifics of the factors that characterise solicitor-centred and client-centred firms, but rather the nature of the underlying picture and the extent to which this reflects the prevailing attitudes, cultures and methods of operating within your own firm. Having done this, and having identified which end of the spectrum the firm is biased towards currently, think about *why* the firm is where it is. More often than not, you will find that the nature of the firm mirrors the general approach of the one or two longest serving and most senior of the partners.

SUMMARY

Within this chapter we have focused upon some of the dimensions of a client-centred firm and how such an approach can only be developed against the background of a clear and detailed understanding of clients' expectations. In developing a stronger client orientation, an obvious starting point is the recognition of the distinction between features and benefits and of the need to look outside the firm and evaluate its offer from the clients' perspective. In the absence of this, the firm will almost inevitably lack the client focus that increasingly is being demanded and expected.

CHAPTER 4

Client satisfaction and the role of marketing research

> Having read this chapter, you should:
> - understand the nature and purpose of marketing research;
> - appreciate how it might contribute to the management of the firm;
> - understand how marketing research can be used to measure levels of client satisfaction;
> - be aware of the factors that need to be taken into account in designing a survey of clients; and
> - be capable of designing a straightforward and useable questionnaire.

When the history of the twentieth century comes to be written, the one thing that is certain is that the 1980s and 90s will be labelled decades of change. The effects of this have been felt in a wide variety of ways, since people today are not only generally more knowledgeable (something which to a harried receptionist on a busy Monday morning may not always necessarily be particularly obvious) but also far more willing to complain (often painfully obvious) than was typically the case in the past. Partly because of changes such as these, but also because clients are much more willing to vote with their feet by moving to another firm if they feel dissatisfied, the need to measure levels of client satisfaction – and act upon the results – is now greater than ever before. However, in doing this you should not focus just upon the question of how clients interact with the firm, but you should instead take a broader approach so that account is also taken of how your clients interact with specialists such as barristers and other experts when you refer them on for more focused advice and assistance, even though of course you remain the point of client contact.

OBTAINING CLIENT FEEDBACK

Although the idea of getting feedback from clients may well seem attractive since it should provide an insight to what the firm is doing right, what it is doing wrong and what changes might be needed, several questions need to be considered before setting out to conduct any sort of client survey. These include:
1. Why are you really bothering to measure satisfaction levels?
2. Whose views will you canvass?
3. How frequently will it be done? Will it, for example, be a one-off exercise or something which is done on a regular basis?
4. Who will analyse the results?
5. Who will see the results?
6. How will the results be used?

Although the answers to some of these questions might appear at first sight to be glaringly obvious, they are asked in all seriousness. In working with a number of firms, we have come across several in which surveys of clients have been conducted seemingly because they appeared to be a good idea rather than with any real thought having been given to how the results might be used. In other firms we have found that surveys have been conducted and suggestions made, only for one or more of the partners to dismiss the results as meaningless or to argue that the cost of making any of the changes that are called for is too high.

There are several possible lessons to be learned from these sorts of experiences. The first is that before doing anything there must be agreement on the part of the partners and staff that a survey will be carried out and that the results – good, bad or indifferent – will not only be taken seriously, but will also be used as a basis for future action. Without this there is no real point in going any further. It also needs to be agreed that the results will be aggregated to ensure confidentiality and used positively rather than negatively. In one case we came across, for example, a client made a critical comment about one of the reception staff which ultimately found its way into the person's annual appraisal. The result was that when the idea of a survey update emerged several months later, the level of support from a large number of the staff was, quite understandably, virtually non-existent.

Although this sort of experience might appear unusual and possibly far fetched, the example has a serious purpose and highlights the need for recognition to be given to the fact that survey results can, on occasions, be uncomfortable and that if surveys of clients are to be conducted, they need to be conducted properly and the results used intelligently and sensitively.

The idea of a survey should, however, be less alien to law firms following the introduction of Practice Rule 15 with its requirement for a clear complaints procedure. Since firms should now have a system in place to handle and collate complaints, a client survey should be looked upon as the 'early warning system' of the complaints process and as a means of identifying potential trouble spots that can then spark off the action which will possibly avert a full complaint at a later stage. It is, of course, far better to have the chance to deal with trouble before it disrupts the firm's performance and possibly leads to the loss of clients and generates bad publicity.

APPROACHES TO RESEARCH

In deciding how to collect clients' views, you have a choice between a series of formal and informal methods. The informal, which include occasional talks with clients, anecdotes and gossip, have little if any real value, since almost invariably they lack the objectivity that you are looking for and indeed need. Undoubtedly, however, in some firms it is these sorts of techniques which predominate and which then provide the basis for subsequent decisions.

The alternative to this is a series of rather more formal methods which offer far greater scope for gaining an objective and far more detailed insight to clients' views. The best known of these formal methods are small discussion groups (sometimes called focus groups), evaluation cards and questionnaire-based client surveys; suggestion boxes, however good and cheap they might appear as a way of getting feedback from clients, only rarely prove to be worthwhile.

THE ROLE OF DISCUSSION GROUPS

Discussion groups are now a well-established part of any market researcher's toolkit and involve a group of eight or so people sitting around a table to discuss a particular issue in depth such as their expectations of the solicitor-client relationship and how their current experiences match these expectations.

Although groups such as these are of potential value and can generate a considerably detailed insight, they are time consuming (a single group might conceivably last for between one and two hours), often involve a substantial amount of effort in order to ensure that representative groups of clients appear on time, and require a quiet and undisturbed room as well as a skilled interviewer who is sensitive to the dynamics of the group. On top of all this, it is normal for a token payment (£20 or a bottle of wine) to be made to the participants.

Partly because of the ways in which the costs of running discussion groups can quickly add up, but also because of the specialised – and expensive – skills needed to run a discussion group effectively, many firms see evaluation cards and periodic questionnaire-based surveys to be far more flexible and cost-effective methods of obtaining feedback from clients.

EVALUATION CARDS

The thinking behind evaluation cards, an example of which appears in figure 4.1, is straightforward and based on the idea that by asking clients to answer, say, five or six simple questions on the way out of the office after the interview the firm can monitor standards and perceptions on a low-cost and ongoing basis.

DESIGNING A SURVEY

As an alternative to evaluation cards, which by their very nature can give you only a limited amount of information, periodic and more detailed surveys of clients offer considerably greater scope for monitoring attitudes to and perceptions of a far wider range of features within the firm, as well as highlighting the impact of any changes and any progress that is being made (an example of a questionnaire appears at the end of the chapter in figure 4.3).

However, before rushing away to begin the work of designing a questionnaire-based survey, several factors need to be borne in mind, including:
- completing all but the very briefest of questionnaires takes time;
- clients may well feel stressed and/or preoccupied;
- the point at which the questionnaire is answered (*e.g.* before or after an interview) is likely to influence the pattern of answers; and
- clients may give you the answers that they think you want.

Other rather more practical issues which need to be taken into account include the need for a table, chair and pen at which self-completion questionnaires can be answered or, if the questions are being asked and the answers recorded by an interviewer, an area in which the client's answers and comments will not be overheard.

Figure 4.1 A sample evaluation card

As a firm we are committed to improving the service and facilities that we offer to our clients. To help with this, we should be grateful if you would spend a few minutes answering the questions below. ALL RESULTS ARE TREATED IN ABSOLUTE CONFIDENCE.

1 Did you have any problems making a convenient appointment?   Yes / No

2 Were the reception staff helpful?   Yes / No

3 Were you seen by the solicitor at the appointment time?   Yes / No

4 Do you feel that the solicitor spent enough time with you?   Yes / No

5 Do you fully understand the solicitor's advice and instructions?   Yes / No

6 Do you feel that you have been kept fully informed of the progress of your case? Yes / No

7 Do you have any suggestions as to how we might possibly improve our service?

Thank you for spending time completing this questionnaire.

Nevertheless, despite these minor obstacles and difficulties, surveys – if conducted properly – can be of enormous value, particularly if a series of basic guidelines (which at first sight might appear obvious but all too easily tend to be forgotten in the excitement of compiling a questionnaire) are adhered to; these are illustrated in figure 4.2.

Figure 4.2 The ten guidelines for designing effective questionnaires

1 Keep questions short.

2 Make sure that the questions are simple and unambiguous.

3 Don't ask questions which lead respondents to a particular answer.

4 Try not to ask too many questions (ten is a reasonable number, twelve or thirteen is probably the absolute maximum in these circumstances).

5 Allow respondents to be anonymous.

6 Avoid potentially embarrassing questions.

7 Wherever possible, use questions which allow respondents either to give simple 'Yes/No' answers or use a rating scale, since they make the job of analysis far easier. Open ended questions (*e.g.* 'Do you have any suggestions for how the range of services might be improved?') can give interesting answers but often take a great deal of time to analyse. If therefore you feel that open ended questions would be useful, try to use as few as possible.

8 Work out in advance how the results will be analysed and used (a tip worth remembering is that students from a local university, particularly if they are on a Business Studies course, may well be able to help in the development of a questionnaire, as well as in the analysis of the results and preparation of the report).

9 Include a section at the end of the questionnaire which will allow you to classify respondents by age, sex, marital status, type of client or any other dimension which is considered to be significant.

10 Having designed the questionnaire, 'pilot' it on a small number of clients to check that any ambiguities and other problems can be ironed out.

WHO SHOULD THE SURVEY COVER?

With regard to the question of who precisely should be covered by the survey, the answer depends to a very large extent upon the nature of your client profile and the survey's objectives. In some cases, the nature of the sample is self evident. Where, for example, you are interested in the views of clients who have been successful in making a claim for compensation in a personal injury case, the question of who to approach is not difficult to determine. For a study which has a rather broader purpose, such as identifying general levels of satisfaction with appointment times, reception areas, and so on, a representative cross-section of clients will be needed.

With regard to the numbers of people who will be covered by the study, a key constraint is often that of the amount of time and effort involved in the analysis. Although on the face of it, the administration and analysis of two hundred completed questionnaires may seem manageable, remember that if each questionnaire consists of just ten questions, this will lead to two thousand answers that will need to be looked at and analysed, all of which will typically have to be done by a partner or the office or practice manager on top of his or her normal day-to-day pressures. Because of this, a rather more pragmatic approach would involve dealing with, say, thirty or forty questionnaires a week for four or five weeks or, as we suggested earlier, using a student to do the work for you.

AFTER THE SURVEY

Having conducted the survey, the question that you then have to face is that of how the results will be presented to the staff. Insofar as it is possible to give advice on this, it has to be that you should be as open as possible. Your staff will only be too aware that a survey of clients has been conducted and want to know what has been said. Given this, you should aim to produce a summary of the key findings – positive as well as negative – within a week or so of the survey being completed and circulate this to everyone in the firm, together with an outline of how the results will be used in the future management of the firm. As part of this you ought to think about picking out a sample of the good responses and putting them on the noticeboard (if you have not got one, this is a good time to put one up). Not only does the fee earner/secretary who acted for the client get to know about it, so do others within the office.

SUMMARY

Within this chapter, we have focused upon some of the ways in which you might obtain feedback from clients and measure the levels of satisfaction that exist. Against the background of what has been said, you might usefully consider the following questions:

1. If you were to go ahead with a survey of clients, who would have the responsibility for managing the survey by developing the questionnaire, analysing the results and preparing the report?
2. What information do you feel you really need to manage the firm more effectively?
3. What do you feel would be the best ways in which to collect this information?
4. How will you present the results to the staff?

Figure 4.3 An example of a client satisfaction questionnaire

As a firm, we are committed to improving the range of facilities and the quality of the service that we offer to our clients. To help us with this, we should be grateful if you would spend a few minutes completing this questionnaire.

ALL RESULTS WILL BE TREATED IN ABSOLUTE CONFIDENCE.

Please give a rating to each of the following elements of the firm by putting a tick in the appropriate box.

	Good	Adequate	Bad
1 The appointments system and:			
(a) getting through by telephone to make an appointment	☐	☐	☐
(b) being able to make an appointment at a time that is convenient to you	☐	☐	☐
(c) the solicitor's punctuality	☐	☐	☐
2 The receptionists and their:			
(a) helpfulness	☐	☐	☐
(b) friendliness	☐	☐	☐
(c) efficiency	☐	☐	☐

(continued)

	Good	Adequate	Bad

3 The waiting room and its:
   (a) level of comfort ☐ ☐ ☐
   (b) range of facilities ☐ ☐ ☐
   (c) cleanliness ☐ ☐ ☐
   (d) tidiness ☐ ☐ ☐

4 The interview with the solicitor and:
   (a) the amount of time spent with you ☐ ☐ ☐
   (b) the solicitor's friendliness ☐ ☐ ☐
   (c) the solicitor's helpfulness ☐ ☐ ☐

	Yes	No

5 Having seen the solicitor, do you fully understand the advice given? ☐ ☐

	Good	Adequate	Bad

6 How do you rate the quality of letters and other documentation you receive from us? ☐ ☐ ☐

	Yes	No

7 Has the solicitor ever referred you to a barrister for further advice? ☐ ☐

If yes please go to question 8
If no please go to question 9

	Good	Adequate	Bad

8 How would you rate the barrister and his / her:
   (a) helpfulness ☐ ☐ ☐
   (b) friendliness ☐ ☐ ☐
   (c) efficiency? ☐ ☐ ☐

9 Taking all of these factors into account, how would you rate the overall quality of the service that you have received from us? ☐ ☐ ☐

(continued)

10 Do you have any suggestions as to how we might possibly improve the service we offer to you?

11 Now please give a few details about yourself:
    Sex: male   ☐
                 female   ☐
    Age: 18-29   ☐
                 30-39   ☐
                 40-49   ☐
                 50-64   ☐
                 65+   ☐

12 How frequently have you visited these offices?
    This is my first visit   ☐
    Once before   ☐
    Between two and five times   ☐
    More than five times   ☐

Thank you for completing this questionnaire.

CHAPTER 5

Environmental pressures and the parable of the boiled frog

> Having read this chapter, you should:
> - understand the various dimensions of the macro and micro external environments and how their patterns of interaction are capable of affecting the firm;
> - understand the need to review the environment on a regular basis;
> - appreciate how the environment creates opportunities and threats;
> - have an insight to the ways in which the firm's environment is likely to develop and become more volatile over the next few years; and
> - understand the implications of this for approaches to the firm's organisation.

We commented in Chapter 2 that marketing involves a four-stage process: environmental analysis; planning; implementation; and feedback and control. Within this chapter we focus upon the first of these and examine the significance of the firm's environment, the ways in which it is changing, the implications of this and how an understanding of the probable patterns of environmental change is capable of contributing to more effective marketing planning. However, before looking at the detail of this, it is worth learning the lesson of the boiled frog.

THE PARABLE OF THE BOILED FROG

All organisations are faced with a series of environmental changes and challenges. The principal difference between the effective and the ineffective organisation is how well it responds, something that was encapsulated several years ago in one of the most popular of management fables, the parable of the boiled frog. What is now referred to as 'the boiled frog syndrome' is based on the idea that if you drop a frog into a pan of hot water, it instantly leaps out. If, however, you put a frog into a pan of lukewarm water and turn the heat up very slowly, it sits there quite happily not noticing the change in its environment. The frog, of course, eventually dies. The parallels with the management and development of any organisation are, or should be, obvious. Faced with sudden and dramatic environmental change, the need for a response is obvious. Faced with a much slower pace of change, the pressures to respond are far less (this is the 'we are doing reasonably well and can reassess things at some time in the future' phenomenon), with the result that the organisation becomes increasingly distant from the real demands of its customers (clients) and other stakeholders. Given this, think seriously about whether you are one of the frogs that is sitting quite happily in a pan of increasingly hot water. If so, why, what are the possible consequences and what, if anything, are you going to do about it?

ANALYSING THE FIRM'S ENVIRONMENT

Although a variety of frameworks have been developed to help in the process of analysing the environment and assessing its probable effect upon an organisation, the most useful of these is referred to as PEST analysis, with PEST representing an acronym of what are the four major dimensions of the environment for the majority of organisations: the **P**olitical/legal; **E**conomic/competitive; **S**ocio-cultural; and **T**echnological elements.

The thinking that underpins PEST analysis is straightforward and involves taking each of the four elements in turn, identifying the nature and significance of any changes that are likely to take place either in the short or in the long term, and then assessing what effect these will have upon the organisation. Having done this, thought can then be given to the actions and responses that are possible and/or demanded.

Although the relative importance of the four factors is likely to vary over time, and indeed their impact may be either direct or indirect, the benefits of regular environmental analysis can be considerable and are reflected most obviously in terms of a firm that is capable of behaving far more proactively, recognising emerging opportunities and threats at a much earlier stage and taking the action that is needed in order to capitalise on the opportunities and minimise – or avoid altogether – the impact of any threats.

It follows from this that if you are to act in a proactive manner, you need to begin by identifying and categorising those parts of the environment over which you are able to exert at least some small degree of control, and those which, by virtue of being totally outside your control, need to be seen as environmental constraints. Some assistance is already available in the form of the Law Society publication 'Succeeding in the 90s' which looks at the strategy proposed by the Law Society not only for itself but also for firms of different sizes. Contained within the document is material for a PEST analysis.

The Citizens Advice Bureaux also often produce profiles of the local community and an assessment of the environment, together with a commentary on likely trends. Information that can help when conducting a PEST analysis is also likely to be available through the local Chambers of Commerce, TEC or Business Link office.

Having carried out an analysis of the environment, you can then start to develop a strategy which is far more likely to reflect environment pressures and realities rather than the partners preconceived – and possibly misconceived – ideas of what is feasible.

The reality for many firms is, of course, that the vast majority of external factors are constraints which only rarely can be changed or influenced to any real degree. The implications of this are, firstly, that the argument for monitoring the environment is inescapable since you need to shape the firm so that it more accurately reflects environmental demands, and secondly, that you need to structure the firm so that it is sufficiently flexible to be able to respond effectively and quickly to external pressures, be they in the form of opportunities or threats.

THE STRUCTURE OF THE ENVIRONMENT

The various dimensions of the environment are illustrated in figure 5.1. It can be seen from this that the environment is capable of being categorised not just on the basis of the PEST factors that we have already referred to, but also on the basis of their macro nature in that they affect the nation as a whole (an obvious example would be changing demographic patterns and in particular the increasing numbers of elderly people needing advice and wills), and their micro impact in that they have a direct and immediate impact upon the firm or the local community; an example of this would be the way in which an upsurge in local levels of unemployment often has a knock on effect upon patterns of crime in the communities affected.

Figure 5.1 The firm's environment

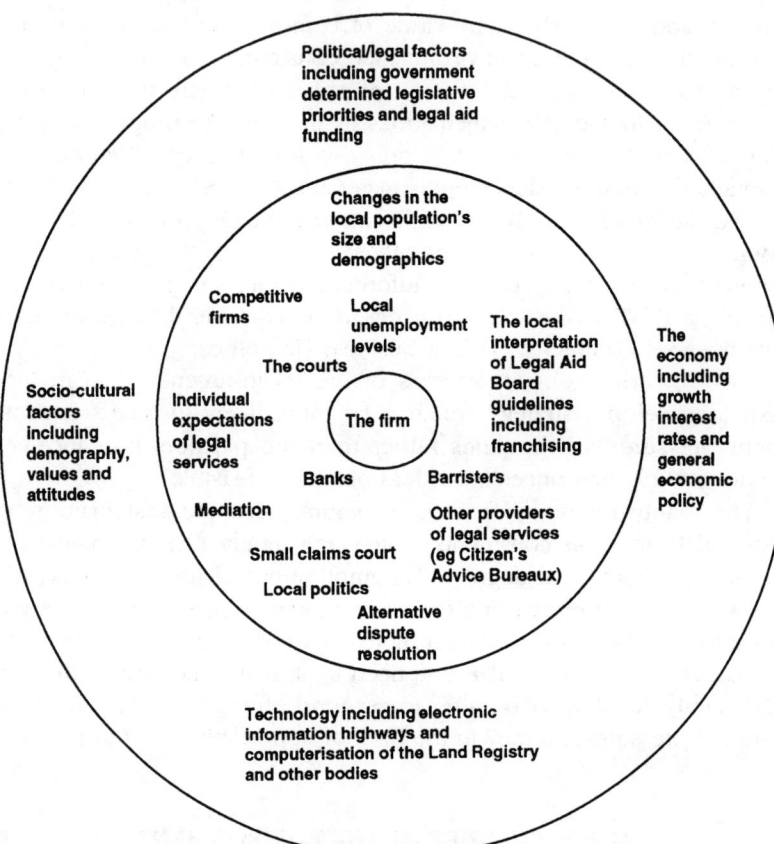

Environmental pressures and the parable of the boiled frog

Because of the ways in which the environment is the immediate or ultimate influence upon patterns of demand for the firm's services, a regular environmental review is capable of providing significant insights not just into the sort of changes taking place but also into the patterns of response and development within the firm that are needed. Without this, it is likely that sooner or later the firm will be forced into a series of reactive responses in a desperate attempt to avoid the sort of mismatch between what various parts of the environment are demanding and what the firm is actually offering; this mismatch is illustrated in figure 5.2.

Figure 5.2 The mismatch between environmental demands and the firm

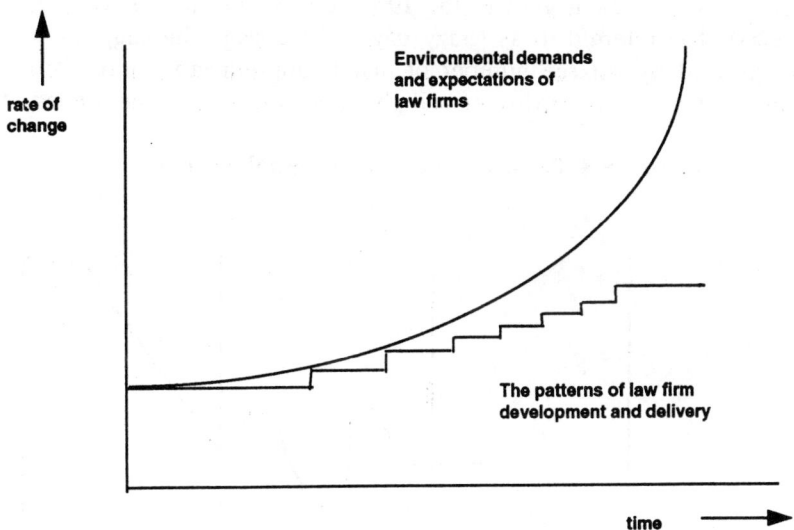

The phenomenon that figure 5.2 illustrates is sometimes referred to as 'strategic drift' and is one that we have encountered in a substantial number of the professional practices that we have dealt with and is manifested in a variety of ways. Among these are growing levels of client dissatisfaction, a failure on the part of the partners to recognise and agree how emerging opportunities might be exploited, little desire amongst the staff to carry out anything other than routine tasks, and a general weakening in the image of the firm both within the community and the profession itself. Faced with this, the only response that is then possible is a radical reassessment of what the environment is demanding of the firm currently, how this is likely to change and how the firm intends responding in order to catch up.

PATTERNS OF ENVIRONMENTAL CHANGE

In looking at any environment, we can categorise it on the basis of the nature and pace of the changes taking place and the managerial/organisational implications of this. In figure 5.3 we illustrate four broad patterns of environmental change: stability; gradual and largely predictable change; a state of flux; and what Tom Peters, the leading American management guru of the 1980s and, at the time of writing, the 1990s has referred to as 'crazy days'. This stage, he suggests is characterised by a large number of major, unpredictable and often seemingly malevolent environmental changes. Crazy days, he argues,

Figure 5.3 Patterns of environmental change

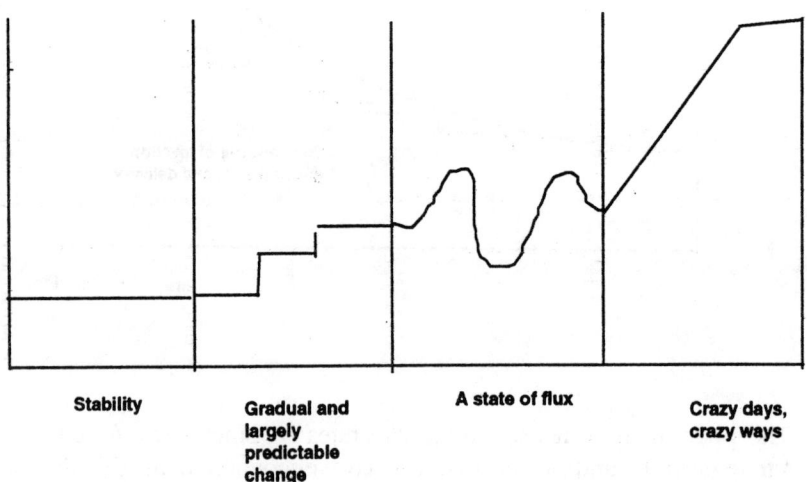

call for very different patterns of management responses in which traditional approaches and mind sets are of little value. It is these new and far more innovative approaches to management that he labels 'crazy ways'.

In the case of law firms, the sort of environmental change faced by lawyers for a long time corresponded to stage two, that of gradual and largely predictable patterns that could be accommodated with few real problems. Over the past few years, however, it is not only the pace and scale of change that has increased dramatically, but also the degree of unpredictability. Because of this, the nature and pace of the responses that are required have escalated enormously, a recent example being the speed at which the Law Society had to produce the Practice Management Standards when pressured by the Legal Aid Board. In organisational and managerial terms, the implications of this can be examined under a number of headings, but particularly in terms of the need for greater organisational flexibility, better patterns of communication and far higher levels of staff training.

THE SIGNIFICANCE OF SOCIAL CHANGE

Perhaps the most significant series of changes that law firms will have to come to terms with over the next few years stem from the series of structural and attitudinal shifts that are taking place within society. Included within these are:
- the growing number of elderly people and a series of other major demographic shifts;
- a general increase in drug abuse and related crime, as well as an upsurge in crime generally;
- an increasing disregard for law and authority;
- rising divorce rates;
- a continuing growth in the service sector, despite the recession;
- the globalisation of markets particularly through the European Union;
- increasing geographic mobility;
- a greater awareness of environmental demands, health and safety issues, and consumer rights;
- changing attitudes to institutional responses and a desire for more personal and individual treatment;
- a greater willingness to complain and seek compensation; and
- expectations of higher service levels at a lower cost.

Although this is not an exhaustive list, it provides an indication of the sorts of social changes that are likely to have an impact over the next few years. Because of this, you should go through the list, adding to it where necessary, and assess the extent to which you feel that your firm will be affected by each of the points and then how you might respond most effectively.

Together, however, they spell out the need for more flexible and organic approaches to law firm organisation. The alternative, a largely traditional and mechanistic structure, simply creates problems. Consider therefore, the questions that appear in figure 5.4.

Figure 5.4 How effectively has your firm responded to and managed change?

1 What are the biggest changes that you feel have affected law firms over the last few years?
2 Which of the changes that have taken place have had the greatest effect upon:
 (a) your firm; and
 (b) you as a member of the firm?
3 Overall, how well do you think that these changes have been handled?
4 What have been the major problems that have been experienced in responding to and managing these changes?
5 What are the principal causes of these problems?
6 What, if anything, has been done and is being done to overcome these problems?
7 What do you see to be the major changes that the firm will have to face up to over the next few years?
8 How well equipped is the firm to deal with these effectively?
9 What areas of managerial strength and weakness exist in the firm?
10 What messages do they send out about your ability to handle future change effectively?

In answering these, you need to give serious thought not just to the superficial changes that have been initiated, but to the rather more fundamental issues of the attitude and behaviour of everyone (partners and staff) in the firm. We know of some firms, for example, which have installed impressive computer systems, changed the titles of some of the staff and even moved to new premises, but which still think and act in the same way that they have for years with no real improvement in their organisation, style of leadership or approaches to teamworking. They are now suffering the problems of poorer performance and substantially worse staff morale, something which has lead us to identify the four different types of firm that are illustrated in figure 5.5.

Figure 5.5 The four types of legal firm and their responses to change

The dinosaurs
These are the firms which exist in a time warp. Life goes on as it always has, with few if any changes. In essence, it is the sort of firm which clients, when sitting in the waiting room, have the chance to read the article in Reader's Digest or National Geographic which they missed on its first time round in 1953. The floors are covered with linoleum, the walls are painted a shade of hospital green that is guaranteed to induce a sense of impending doom in even the most cheerful of clients, the reception staff see the reception area as their personal fiefdom, clients are an unwelcome intrusion and friendliness is seen as a sign of weakness, whilst the solicitors regret the changes that have led to quill pens no longer being a central part of document production. The competition from other firms of solicitors is generally either ignored (competition from the paralegals is beyond the pale) or dismissed on the grounds that the partners are too young and/or flashy. The client base is small and declining and made up primarily of the elderly who have been with the firm for years and who would find the transfer to another firm impossible even to contemplate. Change is seen as a nuisance, a threat and largely unnecessary, with the result that the partners work hard to avoid any move away from the methods of operation which were at the cutting edge of law firm management in the 1920s.

The docile and contented cows that are ambling along
These are the firms that have made steady if unspectacular incremental progress. The waiting room has been spruced up, the magazines are circa 1981, the staff have name badges, a computer has been installed, the inputting of data has begun and the partners regularly attend Law Society events in order to find out about the latest legal and management advances. However, the partners are waiting to discover the outcome of the next general election before deciding whether to take on legal aid franchising. The decision should coincide with the first real outputs from the computer.

The sheep
This is the sort of firm in which the senior partner has latched on to and introduced every new idea that has come along in the last five years only to replace it after a couple of months with something new. There is little evidence of planning or of a well thought out and sustained direction for the firm, but considerable evidence of a series of knee-jerk responses to a variety of half-baked ideas. The computer system is impressive. The waiting room is immediately recognisable by its abstract paintings, the glass and chrome furniture, old copies of some fairly esoteric management journals, and the prominently displayed – and, it must be said, largely meaningless and incomprehensible – practice mission statement which makes reference to breaking down barriers between clients and staff and the development of far stronger and truly meaningful interpersonal relationships, even though they are quite conspicuously not working.

The senior partner in these practices is easily identified by a wild-eyed look and messianic approach that is tempered by a growing realisation that none of the numerous management innovations that have been introduced is really working in the hoped for or promised way. Other staff in the firm are recognisable by their air of weary resignation and a sense of impending doom.

The legal eagles
These are the firms in which considerable thought has been given to the future and to the sorts of objectives that are most appropriate. These thoughts have then been reflected in a series of considered and appropriate responses that take full account of the various stakeholders' expectations. The result is a firm that is well prepared to cope with the challenges of the next few years and in which complacency, partner rivalry, obstruction and self-satisfaction have no place.

The firm is recognisable for its quiet efficiency as soon as you walk through the door. The reception area is staffed by people wearing the firm's uniform and a name badge who know how to put you at your ease and seem genuinely to care. They know most of the clients by their name and make sure that the office runs efficiently. The waiting area is light and airy, has comfortable chairs, a selection of recent magazines, an up-to-date notice board and an ample supply of leaflets providing advice on legal matters. The appointments system works to time and clients are never hurried in or out of the interview rooms. Morale is high, the staff are motivated and, once appointed, rarely leave.

Although there is an obvious element of parody in at least two of these profiles, there is a more serious underlying question which is concerned with the attitudes to change that exist within the firm, how well the firm has responded to change so far, the extent to which planning for the future is going on, and the quality of this planning. The question of how well the firm has responded so far was touched upon in figure 5.4 and may well have highlighted issues of whether the responses to change have been planned or largely fortuitous. With regard to the issue of the quality of planning for the future, you need to give thought to two interrelated issues: firstly, the extent to which there is a fundamental recognition on the part of the solicitors and support staff of the need to continue changing over the next few years and, secondly, the willingness to make these changes rather than simply responding to them. This is illustrated in figure 5.6.

Having placed the firm within this matrix, ask yourself a few straightforward questions:
- Why are we in this cell of the matrix?
- Are we happy with this? If so what do we have to do either to stay here or improve yet further?
- If we are not happy with the current position, what are the root causes and what do we have to do to improve things?

WAYS OF IMPROVING EACH OF THE TYPES OF LAW FIRM

Given the nature of the profiles in figure 5.5 and your responses to the three questions above, you need to think about how your firm, be it dinosaur or legal eagle, might possibly develop over the next few years. In the case of the *dinosaurs,* there is little that will really achieve any change short of the senior partner retiring and the receptionist leaving a few days later because "standards will never be the same again." However, even then, because the client base is small and declining and made up primarily of elderly people, anyone who takes over the practice is faced with a major uphill struggle to modernise the premises and attract a bigger and younger client base. Like the dinosaurs of the past, the dinosaur law firms of today are destined simply to die and will reappear only in museums as a reminder of what things used to be like.

The docile and contented cows that currently are ambling along have a slightly brighter future, although just how bright this proves to be is likely to depend upon the arrival of a shining knight on horseback

Figure 5.6 The change matrix

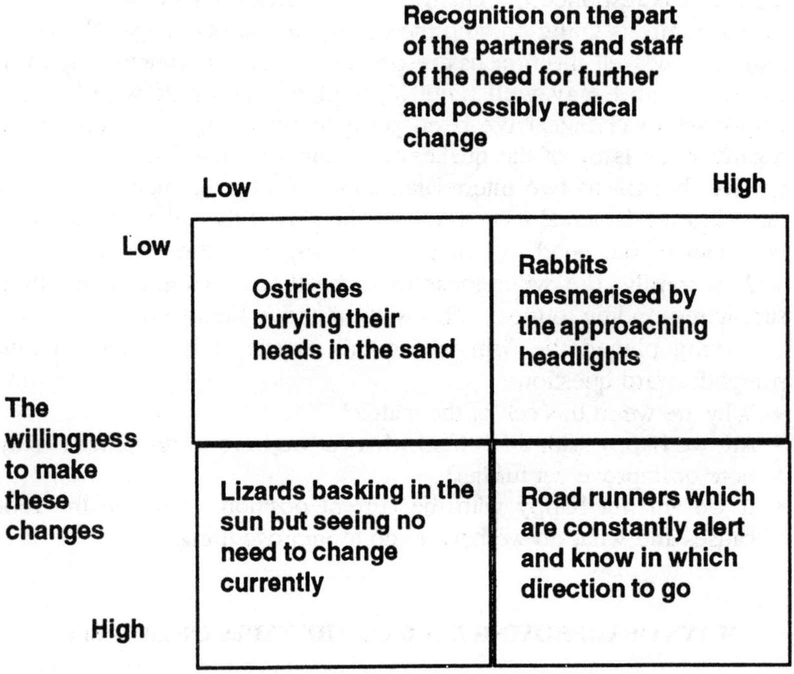

	Recognition on the part of the partners and staff of the need for further and possibly radical change	
	Low	**High**
Low The willingness to make these changes **High**	Ostriches burying their heads in the sand	Rabbits mesmerised by the approaching headlights
	Lizards basking in the sun but seeing no need to change currently	Road runners which are constantly alert and know in which direction to go

(apologies for mixing the metaphors). Without the injection of some new ideas, many of which are likely to prove uncomfortable, the contented cows will continue to amble along and eventually will illustrate radical new thinking on evolution by taking on the shape of the *dinosaurs*.

In many ways, *the sheep* represent the most interesting challenge, since in these firms the senior partner's approach is a case study of exactly how in managerial terms you shouldn't do things. The range of solutions here is therefore relatively small and limited either to a palace coup (look to South American politics and the guidance given by the CIA for exactly how this might be done) or an appeal to decency (the British army in the nineteenth century wrote the rule book on this one by giving a loaded revolver to anyone who let the side down, pointing them in the direction of a darkened room and encouraging them to do the decent thing). Either way, it comes down to what most personnel managers refer to as "a major career change time" or "an opportunity to pursue other interests."

With regard to the *legal eagles* and how they might improve on what is already a pretty slick operation, there is little that can be said. Insofar as they might possibly have a problem, it is that they run the risk of achieving the very high standards that they are aiming for and then becoming complacent. However, the true eagles recognise this, guard against it and fly ever higher.

THE STEPS IN ANALYSING THE ENVIRONMENT

In figure 5.7, we provide a framework that is designed to help in the process of identifying how the environment is likely to change over the next few years, what the implications for the firm are likely to be, and what the strategic imperatives are (a strategic imperative is a 'must do' factor in that if you fail to address it, the consequences for the firm are likely to be significant). Having done this, you can then move on to figures 5.8-5.11 which require you to look more specifically at the four principal dimensions of the environment that we referred to earlier (Political, Economic, Social and Technological), identify the changes taking place, assess whether these represent opportunities or threats, and what action the firm needs to take.

To do this, you need to work your way through each of these areas in turn with your partners and other key members of staff with a view to identifying, firstly, the nature of any changes that are likely to take place and then, secondly, the implications of these for the firm. In

Figure 5.7 Basic environmental beliefs and the strategic imperatives that arise from this

Basic environmental beliefs		
I believe that the following environmental changes will take place over the next few years 1 2 3 4 5 6 7 8 9 10	The implications for the firm of each of these changes will be: 1 2 3 4 5 6 7 8 9 10	The strategic imperatives (the must-dos) that emerge from this are: 1 2 3 4 5 6 7 8 9 10

doing this, use a flipchart and brainstorm so that as many ideas as possible are generated without being evaluated or criticised. (If you are unfamiliar with the technique of brainstorming, the essence of it is that you have a short period during which as many ideas as possible are written up onto the flipchart. The main rule is that criticism is forbidden at this stage, so that people are not afraid to put forward their thoughts, no matter how bizarre they might seem.) Once you have done this, go back and evaluate each of the ideas before entering them in figures 5.8-5.11.

To help in this process of getting started, the questions that appear below might be of some help. Deliberately we have posed just a few questions under each heading with a view to you then developing the list at much greater length and in much greater detail.

The political/legal framework

- What sorts of changes in the current government's policies do you foresee?
- What might a change in government mean for lawyers in general?
- What changes do you foresee in Legal Aid Board priorities?
- What effect would a change in funding levels for legal services have?
- What changes do you foresee in the levels of solicitors' responsibility and accountability?
- What changes seem likely in the incentives given to members of the public to take legal expenses insurance?
- Who within the firm has the responsibility for keeping the partners up to date on relevant changes in the law?

The economic, competitive and provider environments

- What changes do you expect to see in economic conditions both nationally and locally?
- How will unemployment levels move locally and what are the implications for patterns of demand for legal services?
- In what ways is competition becoming more significant for law firms and how is this affecting you?
- What changes are likely to take place amongst other suppliers of legal services such as the Citizens Advice Bureaux, licensed conveyancers and authorised probate practitioners, and what are the implications of each change for law firms?
- What sort of relationship do you have with adjacent firms?

- What appear to be their objectives and how are they likely to develop over the next few years? Does their pattern of development have any implications for you?
- What might you learn from how others firms operate?
- Is there any scope for co-operation? Can you pool resources such as the library, forms or staff (temporary cover for absentees)? Can you refer work on a structured basis for mutual advantage?
- What changes do you expect to see in the relationships with providers such as barristers?

The social and cultural environments

- What social changes do you expect to see over the next few years?
- What are the implications for you of trends and shifts in the local population size and demographic structures?
- In what ways are clients' expectations of law firms changing?
- In what ways are values and lifestyles changing?
- What new social and cultural pressures and priorities are emerging?

The technological environment

- How will technological changes and developments affect solicitors over the next few years?
- In what ways might individual's expectations of higher technology legal solutions develop?
- What are the implications for your office and working methods of new technological developments?
- Are you and your partners fully up to date with the nature and patterns of technological developments in delivery of legal services?
- How might you use new technology to improve your range and level of services?
- Does anyone within the firm have the specific responsibility for monitoring new technological developments and keeping the others informed?

Having gone through this exercise, you should have a far clearer and more focused view of how the firm's environment is likely to develop and what the implications of this are likely to be. Armed with this information, you should then be in a position to begin identifying in detail the sorts of opportunities and threats that exist currently, the ways in which they are most likely to develop in the near future and can best be handled; a framework for this appears in figure framework is developed further both in Chapter 7 and, in , in figures 7.3 and 7.4, and in Chapter 8).

**Figure 5.8 Probable PEST developments
The political/legal environments**

The probable political/legal developments are......	The probable specific effects upon the firm are....	Do these represent an opportunity or a threat?	What do we need to do to capitalise upon each opportunity or minimise the threat?
*	* * *	* * *	* * *
*	* * *	* * *	* * *
*	* * *	* * *	* * *

Figure 5.9 Probable PEST developments
The economic/competitive environments

The probable economic/competitive developments are......	The probable specific effects upon the firm are.....	Do these represent an opportunity or a threat?	What do we need to do to capitalise upon each opportunity or minimise the threat?
*	* * *	* * *	* * *
*	* * *	* * *	* * *
*	* * *	* * *	* * *

**Figure 5.10 Probable PEST developments
The socio-cultural environments**

The probable socio-cultural developments are.......	The probable specific effects upon the firm are....	Do these represent an opportunity or a threat?	What do we need to do to capitalise upon each opportunity or minimise the threat?
*	* * *	* * *	* * *
*	* * *	* * *	* * *
*	* * *	* * *	* * *

Environmental pressures and the parable of the boiled frog

**Figure 5.11 Probable PEST developments
The technological environment**

The probable technological developments are.......	The probable specific effects upon the firm are.....	Do these represent an opportunity or a threat?	What do we need to do to capitalise upon each opportunity or minimise the threat?
*	* * *	* * *	* * *
*	* * *	* * *	* * *
*	* * *	* * *	* * *
*	* * *	* *	* * *

Figure 5.12 The opportunities and threats facing the firm

The opportunities open to us appear to be........	Significance (1=of little significance 5=of major significance)	The actions that are needed to capitalise upon the opportunities are......
* * * * *	* * * *	* * * *
The threats facing us appear to be...	Significance (1-5)	The actions needed to minimise the possible impact of the threats are....
* * * * *	* * * *	* * * *

SUMMARY

Within this chapter we have focused upon the various dimensions of the environment and how an understanding of the environment and the ways in which it is likely to change underpins any worthwhile approach to planning. Against this background, consider the following questions:

1. Do you feel that you have a sufficiently detailed understanding of how the firm's environment is likely to change over the next few years?
2. What sort of environment does it look as if you will have to face up to? (refer back to figure 5.3)
3. How confident are you that you will be able to cope effectively?
4. Where do the greatest opportunities and threats appear to be?
5. Given your previous patterns of behaviour, how are you most likely to respond to any changes? Will it be very largely in the form of a series of almost desperate moves or in a much more systematic and planned manner?
6. Is there currently a mismatch between what your firm is offering and what the market is really demanding? (refer back to figure 5.2) If there is a gap, how significant is it and what are you doing/will you do to close it?

Finally, return for moment to our story of the boiled frog and think not just about the lessons that emerge from this but also, in the light of your responses to the questions that we have raised within this chapter, what sort of frog you *really* are.

CHAPTER 6

Planning for success (part 1): assessing your planning skills

> Having read this chapter, you should:
> - understand more clearly what you want from planning; and
> - have a greater understanding of the planning skills and abilities possessed by you and your colleagues.

SO WHAT DO YOU WANT FROM PLANNING?

It has long been recognised that planning is generally a relatively easy and straightforward exercise and that the development of a truly worthwhile plan takes only a little more time and effort than that involved in preparing one which is mediocre. The problems that many organisations face come therefore not at the planning stage but are instead related to the ways in which the plan is implemented. Far too often, for example, too few resources are put into the process of implementation and responsibilities are only loosely allocated, with the result that objectives are not achieved within the hoped for timescales. Faced with this, the all too common reaction, particularly when the environment is changing rapidly, is to see planning as being of little real value and the process as little more than a hollow exercise.

If, however, the processes of planning and implementation are seen to be interconnected, responsibilities are properly allocated and someone within the firm takes on the task of 'driving' the plan, the benefits can be considerable and reflected in a far tighter focus and much higher levels of motivation and performance.

However, for many managers – and we include solicitors within this – planning runs the risk of taking on what is sometimes loosely referred to as 'motherhood' status. In other words, it is warm, reassuring and

difficult to argue against. Before we go any further, therefore, you need to consider seven simple questions:
1 Why are you bothering to plan?
2 What will the plan be used for?
3 How will it be used?
4 Who will be involved in the planning process?
5 Who will write it (and how)?
6 Who will manage and drive it?
7 What measures of success will you use?

THE TWO APPROACHES TO PLANNING

In working with a wide variety of organisations over the years, it has become apparent that when it comes to planning there are two broad approaches. The first is characterised by an emphasis upon producing a lengthy, detailed, highly polished and professional looking plan which either literally or figuratively is then filed until the start of the next year's planning cycle.

The second approach, and the one to which we want to give emphasis in this chapter, gives full recognition to the benefits of the planning *process* in that it provides a forum for a detailed review of the environment, objectives, priorities, resources, strengths and weaknesses, and to the alternative patterns of proactive development that exist. This is then reflected in the plan itself which represents a *working document* in that it is used on a daily/weekly basis to manage the firm. Given this, the answer to the first of the seven questions that we posed earlier has to be that any plan that is developed must be realistic and designed to make a major contribution to the management of the firm rather than to satisfy any guidelines or expectations of bodies such as the Legal Aid Board or the Law Society. (A rule of thumb that we often use as a first step when talking to solicitors or other professionals about their planning process simply involves looking at the firm's planning document. If it is dog-eared, has been annotated and is relatively slim, the chances are that it is used on a day-to-day basis as a working document. Presented with a fat and pristine plan, we can almost guarantee that the plan is not really used and that we will be able to sell the firm some consultancy advice on how to improve their planning – and implementation – processes.)

It follows from this that you therefore need to think seriously about developing a *planning culture* within the firm in which the process of planning is taken seriously rather than being only a once-a-year ritual.

Planning for success (part 1): assessing your planning skills 73

BEING REALISTIC ABOUT YOUR PLANNING SKILLS

Perhaps one of the most common complaints that we hear from professionals on a regular basis is that they qualified in order to practice their particular discipline rather than to become professional managers. Although we have a certain sympathy for this view, few solicitors today are able to duck their management and planning responsibilities. The Law Society, for example, has already stated its wish that at least 25% of a solicitor's Continuing Professional Development should be in the form of management and skills training, whilst the Legal Aid Franchising scheme already requires firms to conduct some form of planning to arrive at an outline strategy for the development of the firm.

However, recognising that solicitors currently vary enormously in terms of their planning abilities, a first stage in developing an effective planning process involves being realistic (perhaps brutally honest would be a better phrase) about the planning skills of each of the partners within the firm. To do this, begin with the matrix that appears in figure 6.1 which requires you to categorise individuals on the basis of two dimensions: their apparent long term planning abilities and their skills in day-to-day management. Using this matrix, identify where you, your partners and each member of the management team are

Figure 6.1 The short and long term management skills matrix

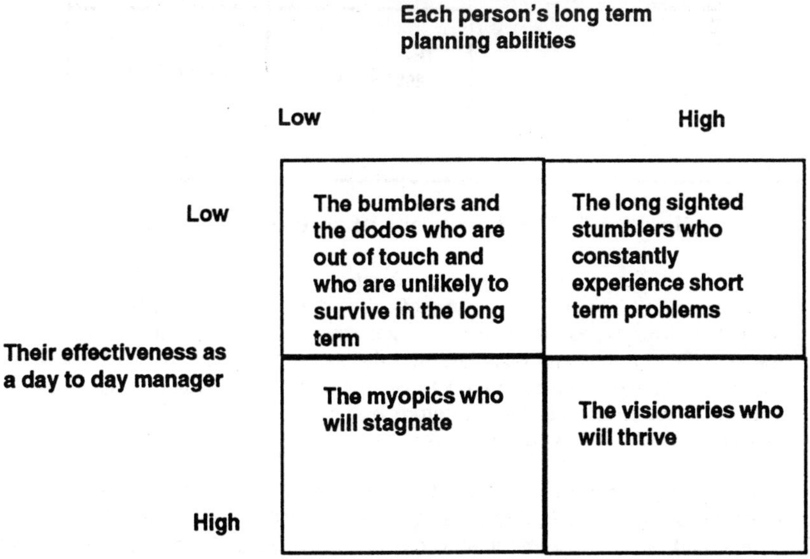

Each person's long term planning abilities

	Low	High
Low (Their effectiveness as a day to day manager)	The bumblers and the dodos who are out of touch and who are unlikely to survive in the long term	The long sighted stumblers who constantly experience short term problems
High	The myopics who will stagnate	The visionaries who will thrive

located. The picture that emerges from this should give you a reasonable insight to the overall quality of management and the planning strengths that exist within the firm, whether there is a need to strengthen these, and who might be best equipped to take on the initial responsibility for planning (this is not necessarily always the senior partner). In completing this matrix, you are also arriving at a measure of what is loosely referred to as organisational capability; that is the firm's capacity for handling change and moving ahead in the right direction.

Against this background, you should then move to figure 6.2 which enables you to categorise yourself and your colleagues on the basis of their *willingness* to manage and their *ability* to manage; the four types that this produces are discussed in figure 6.3.

Figure 6.2 The four management styles

The ability of each person to manage

	Low	High
Low	The incompetent meddlers	The opt-outs and the ostriches
High	The dangerlawyers	The superlawyers

Their willingness to manage

Figure 6.3 The four types of solicitor-manager

In the light of a study that we conducted amongst managers of medical practices in 1993 to find out how they viewed their GPs as managers, we identified four types of doctor-manager: the supermedics, the dangermedics, the opt-outs and ostriches, and the incompetent meddlers. In our work with lawyers, we have found that this categorisation can be applied with an unnerving ease. We therefore leave it to you to work out which most nearly describes your own style.

The *supermedic* proved to be an all too rare – and unnerving – species but is immediately recognisable by an evangelical gleam in his or her eye, an almost pathological commitment to change, a passion for computerisation, and a love of plans, planning and staff information notes. Supermedics tend to put enormous emphasis on mission statements for the practice, partners' away days in order to decide on the future objectives and the shape of the firm, staff motivation, and scrupulous record keeping. Their briefcases bulge with business plans and a mobile phone sits next to the stethoscope.

The *dangermedics* are the GPs, who, despite few obvious managerial skills, are intent on demonstrating to staff throughout the practice that they are in charge and are full of ideas (few of which are original and fewer still are understood). They tend to use management jargon indiscriminately and are intent on bringing about change; in managerial terms they are the equivalent of someone practising as a doctor having failed their Boy Scouts or Girl Guides first aid badge. All too often, the sorts of changes they make and the systems they introduce are either inappropriate or, because of a lack of planning and commitment, fail to achieve the hoped for results. Despite this, they insist on being involved in everything and often feel that their staff have no real skills or abilities. Because of this, they have an almost neurotic compulsion to give orders to anyone and everyone. Like the supermedics, dangermedics can be recognised in a number of ways, but most obviously by the trail of confusion and/or destruction they leave behind and their insistence upon being consulted about every aspect of the firm. Insofar as they have a pet phrase, it is likely to be either "Didn't I tell you about that? I suppose I must have forgotten," or "Why has it gone wrong? Can't anyone around here do anything right?"

Those in the third category – *the opt-out and ostriches* – are something of a disappointment in that although they have a well-developed ability to manage, they either don't see themselves as managers, and consequently leave others to do it, or still haven't come to terms with the ways in which general practice has changed over the past few years. Tolerant of a degree of chaos, they often develop delegation to a fine art. Insofar as they can be recognised by what they say – as opposed to what they don't do – it is likely to be something along the lines of "I didn't come into medicine to be a manager, I just want to get on with being a doctor."

The fourth category – *the incompetent meddlers* – proved to be surprisingly common and a source of enormous frustration for many practice managers. These are the GPs who consistently fail to complete vital records on time, rarely if ever tell the staff what is going on or where they are going, see no need to plan, frequently change their mind for no apparent reason, insist on being consulted (a bit like dangermedics), and either wouldn't recognise a practice plan if it landed on their desk or wouldn't be able to find it amongst the mess of free gifts from reps, unanswered telephone messages, half-eaten sandwiches, and still-to-be-read articles from the medical press.

SUMMARY

Quite deliberately, within this chapter we have tried to adopt a reasonably light-hearted tone in order to drive home an important message and, in the case of figure 6.3, would again say that we have identified uncanny parallels between solicitors and GPs. Given the far greater emphasis upon, and indeed the need for planning in the current climate, it is essential that before going any further you have a clear understanding of the managerial and planning strengths that exist within the firm. Without this understanding, there is a danger that you will start with the assumption that all partners have an equal ability and that the responsibilities both for planning and implementation can be shared equally. If our experiences with numerous managers in a wide variety of organisational types over the past twenty years are at all typical, this is simply not the case. It is the recognition of this and the picture that emerges from the various matrices that we have used in this chapter that leads us to suggest that it is only after you have identified the level and nature of the planning and managerial skills within the firm that the question of who is to be responsible for developing and then subsequently implementing the plan can really be decided.

In summary, therefore, consider the following questions:
1 What overall picture emerges from the various matrices?
2 Does it appear that you have sufficient long term planning skills within the firm? If not, what are the probable consequences of this and what might you do to overcome the problem?

CHAPTER 7

Planning for success (part 2): developing the marketing plan

> Having read this chapter, you should:
> - understand the nature, purpose and benefits of planning;
> - have an appreciation of the sorts of problems that are typically encountered in planning;
> - understand the structure of the marketing plan and the inputs that it requires;
> - be aware of how the assumptions that underpin the plan subsequently act as 'drivers' of the plan;
> - appreciate how stakeholders' needs can and should be taken into account; and
> - have an understanding of the sorts of factors that affect the effectiveness of the plan's implementation.

Against the background of our comments in Chapter 6 and, hopefully, a better understanding of the planning skills and abilities that exist within the firm, we can now turn our attention to the question of how best to prepare an effective marketing plan.

THE THREE DIMENSIONS OF PLANNING

We commented in Chapter 6 that plans often fail because too little attention is paid to issues of implementation. Equally, they fail because the objectives that have been set are either far too ambitious or fail to reflect the realities of the environment and/or the organisation's strengths and capabilities. Recognising this, planning, which is designed to provide the organisation with a sense of direction and

purpose, must take place against the background of a clear and detailed understanding of three principal factors:
1 the nature and demands of the environment;
2 the objectives and expectations of the solicitors and staff;
3 the firm's strengths, weaknesses and overall levels of capability.

THE STRUCTURE OF THE MARKETING PLAN

Although there is no one model of the ideal marketing plan, it is relatively easy to identify the twelve areas that need to be included within any worthwhile and useable planning document; these are illustrated in figure 7.1 and then brought together diagrammatically in figure 7.2.

Figure 7.1 The elements of the marketing plan

1 The summary or overview
2 The situational analysis that includes:
   - the assumptions made about environmental pressures and demands and the assessment of the opportunities and threats that exist currently and which seem likely to emerge during the period covered by the plan
   - the assessment of the firm's strengths and weaknesses, its overall level of capability and the identification of any significant gaps
3 The implications of the analysis of strengths, weaknesses, opportunities and threats
4 The principal assumptions underlying the plan
5 The statement of the mission and the short and long term marketing objectives
6 The statement of the strategy that is to be pursued
7 The detail of the tactical actions needed
8 The allocation of responsibilities and timescales
9 The resource implications of the plan
10 Feedback mechanisms
11 The performance measures that are to be used to assess ongoing performance
12 The procedures for review and control

Planning for success (part 2): developing the marketing plan 79

Figure 7.2 The planning process

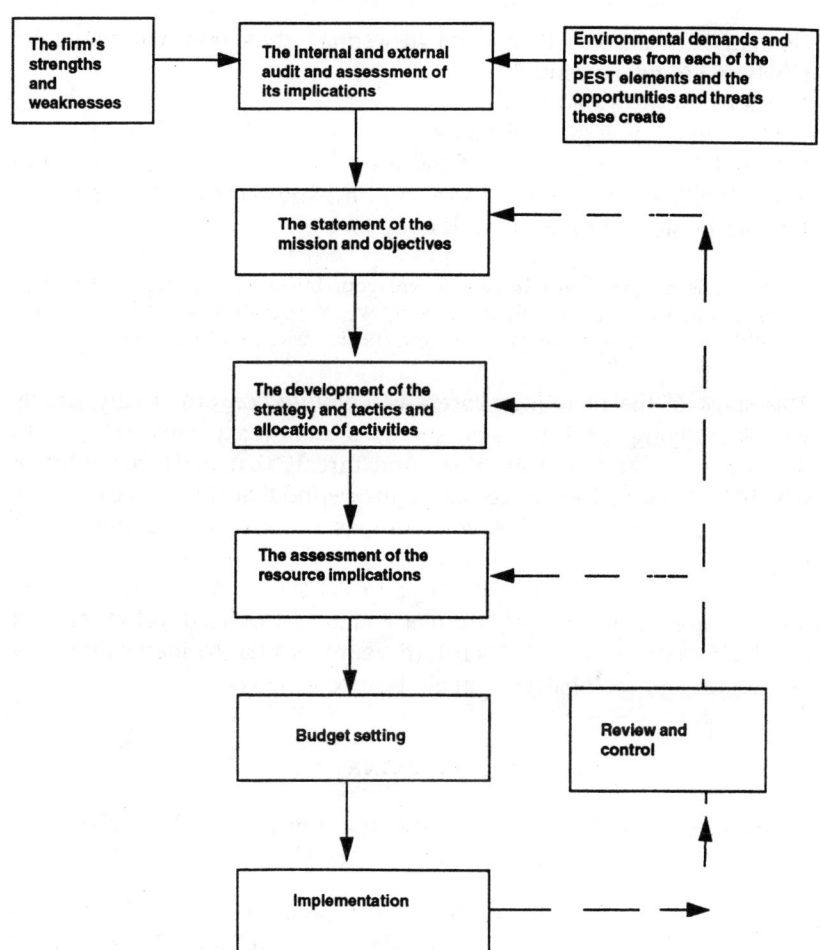

Marketing for Law Firms

DEVELOPING AN EFFECTIVE PLAN

Planning is based on asking – and answering – three principal questions:
1 where are we currently?
2 where do we want to go?
3 how are we going to get there?

The significance of the first of these - where are we currently? - has been highlighted by the ex-chairman of ICI and star of BBC television's Troubleshooter series, Sir John Harvey-Jones:

> "There is no point in deciding where your business is going until you have actually decided with great clarity where you are now. Like practically everything in business, however, this is easier said than done."

This stage of the planning process is therefore concerned very largely with identifying the firm's real strengths and weaknesses, along with the nature of any opportunities and threats that exist currently or which seem likely to emerge during the period that is to be covered by the plan. Having done this, you can then move on to the question of the direction in which you want to take the firm, something which involves the development not just of a clear statement of objectives but also a vision of the sort of firm that you are trying to develop. Against this background, you can then turn your attention to identifying how this vision and the objectives might best be achieved.

STEP ONE

Where are we currently? How to conduct a SWOT analysis that is really worthwhile

SWOT analysis (Strengths, Weaknesses, Opportunities and Threats) has proved to be one of the most commonly used – and abused – managerial and planning tools of the past decade. There are several reasons for this, but perhaps the most obvious is that the technique's apparent simplicity has lulled its users into a false sense of security with the result that all too often the outcome of the analysis is far too bland and meaningless to provide a worthwhile base for planning. Given this, how then can SWOT analysis be made more rigorous and meaningful? The guidelines which emerge from having experienced these sorts of problems with a variety of different types of organisation are straightforward:
- Concentrate upon building a picture of the firm as a whole by carrying out a series of preliminary analyses that focus upon different

parts of the firm such as commercial, litigation, probate and conveyancing departments, and by looking at the particular abilities of key members of staff. In a multi-office firm, for example, you might analyse each separate office. By doing this, you are not only far less likely to miss some of the detail that needs to come from a SWOT, but will also gain a far greater insight into how different parts of the firm are operating and need to develop.
- Do not conduct the analysis on your own, but instead use it as an opportunity for getting the partners and staff from across the firm to pool ideas. It can also be useful to check the views of some professional contacts who may be flattered that you value their opinion and respect your professionalism in undertaking such a thorough exercise.
- Always look at strengths and weaknesses from the viewpoint of the client and other stakeholders. You might even ask certain key clients to give you their views. In this way, you avoid making a series of warm, reassuring and bland motherhood statements about the firm and can concentrate upon identifying how the firm is *really* seen from the outside.
- In looking at strengths and weaknesses, start with a broadly unstructured approach in order to get ideas flowing, but gradually pull the points together under a series of headings so that you can build up a picture of the firm's different dimensions. The sorts of headings that you might use in doing this, include:
  - the solicitors and other fee-earners within the firm
  - the support and administration staff
  - skill levels
  - the premises, including their location
  - the administrative procedures
  - the information technology that is being used
  - financial issues and any investment needs
  - relationships with clients
  - relationships with intermediaries who are in a position to introduce clients to the firm
  - relationships with the Legal Aid Board
  - relationships with suppliers, including barristers and courts
  - the general and specific reputation of the firm
  - any particular outside interests of members of staff that might be used to promote the firm.
- In looking at the external environment, concentrate upon those parts of the environment that are likely to have a direct rather than an indirect effect upon the firm.

- Avoid the temptation simply to list strengths, weaknesses, opportunities and threats, since this tends to lead to what we can refer to as a 'balance sheet' mentality in which you take comfort from the way in which, for example, the number of strengths identified outweighs the number of weaknesses. Instead, spend time evaluating each of the points identified and then rank them in order of importance; a framework for doing this appears in figure 7.3.
- Concentrate upon identifying how the results of the analysis can be used. In the case of strengths, for example, there has to be a matching opportunity; without this, the strength is of little real immediate value. Equally, in the case of weaknesses, think about how each weakness can be overcome or its significance reduced. In the case of threats, again think about how their impact can be neutralised or reduced, and possibly turned into an opportunity; the framework for this appears in figure 7.4.

Figure 7.3 Identifying the firm's strengths, weaknesses, opportunities and threats

Strengths	Significance
Weaknesses	**Significance**
Opportunities	**Significance**
Threats	**Significance**

Figure 7.4 The client oriented SWOT

Developing a vision and a mission for the firm

A considerable amount of management research in recent years has highlighted the importance of vision and mission statements and the role that they are capable of playing in providing staff with a sense of direction and purpose; in the case of law firms, the overall statement of vision would be concerned with a general expression of the sort of firm that the partners are trying to create in the medium to long term. An obvious example of this would be that of a firm which has the strongest reputation locally for the quality of client care and up-to-date facilities (the position of the vision within the planning hierarchy is illustrated in figure 7.5). Such a firm might have a vision statement along the lines of 'to be a high quality general practice providing both legal and financial services to the community within a radius of [10] miles of [Anytown], with a particular emphasis on continuous improvement in standards whilst also achieving maximum profitability'.

You might therefore ask yourself the following question:

> To what extent is there currently a *shared* and *explicit* vision amongst the partners of the sort of firm that we are trying to develop?

In the majority of firms that we have come across, there appears to have been relatively little detailed thought or discussion given to this sort of issue, with the partners having concentrated instead upon a whole series of shorter term issues. It is, however a fundamental part of the planning process, since it represents a collective statement of what in the long term you are really trying to achieve.

Figure 7.5 The planning hierarchy

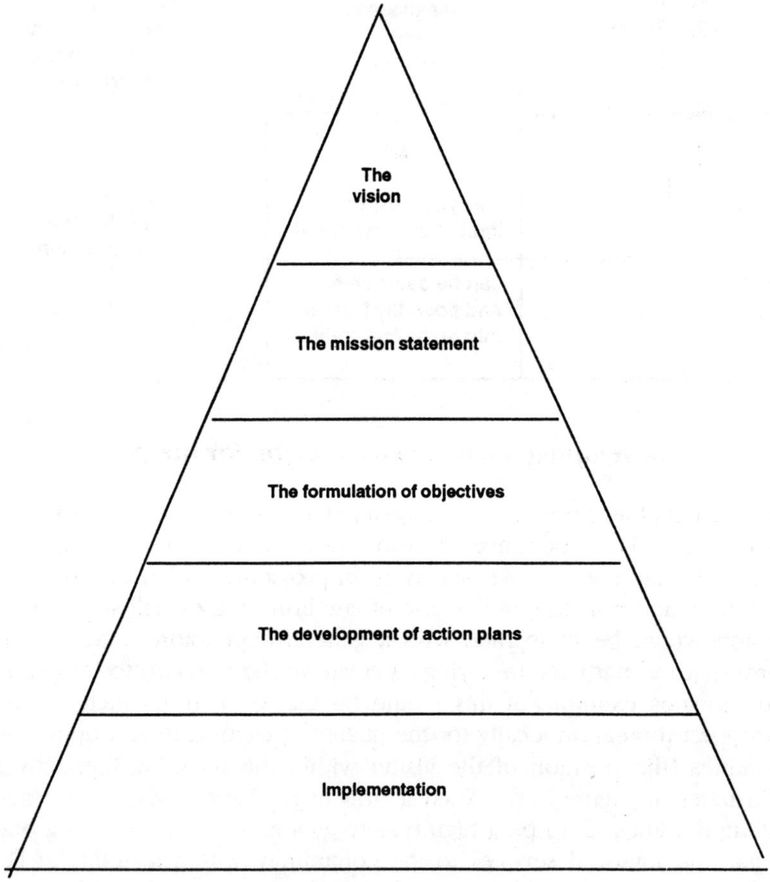

```
              /\
             /  \
            / The \
           / vision \
          /----------\
         /            \
        / The mission  \
       /   statement    \
      /------------------\
     /                    \
    / The formulation of   \
   /      objectives        \
  /--------------------------\
 /                            \
/ The development of action    \
/         plans                 \
/-------------------------------\
/                                \
/        Implementation           \
/----------------------------------\
```

The significance of a shared vision needs to be seen therefore in terms of the broad framework that it is capable of providing and the influence that this should then have both upon the subsequent mission statement and the sorts of objectives that are set.

Given this, think again about the question that we posed earlier (to what extent is there a shared and explicit vision?) and consider raising it at the next partners' meeting with a view to getting an explicit statement

Planning for success (part 2): developing the marketing plan 85

of the sort of firm that, between you, you are trying to create. To help with this, you might usefully also consider the three questions below:
- What do we want the firm to be like and known for in, say, five years time? (In answering this, think not just about legal issues and the reputation, but also the size of the firm, its location and desired level of profitability.)
- How realistic is this vision?
- What do we need to do if we are to translate this vision into reality?

Against this background, you can then move on to the development of the mission statement. A mission statement represents a statement of core values and, again, is part of the framework within which plans are prepared. It is for this reason that at least one commentator has referred to the mission as 'an invisible hand' which guides staff to work in particular ways. There are numerous examples of good mission statements outside law firms, two of which are illustrated in figure 7.6. (Quite deliberately, we have chosen these not from law firms, but from businesses with which you will be familiar on a more general basis.)

Having looked at many hundreds of mission statements over the past few years – some of which have been good, some bad, and others simply a tribute to the ability of the managers to fantasise – there are several lessons that emerge which are worth keeping in mind when developing a mission statement for your firm. They include:
- make sure that it gives a general direction and encompasses key values. It should not include goals or actions
- keep it short, otherwise staff will probably never read it let alone remember it or really understand it
- make sure that it focuses upon fundamental issues and reflects core firm values that will neither need changing nor be changed every six months or so
- make sure that it is believable and not made up of a series of unrealistic 'wish' statements
- make sure that it is exciting and inspirational
- make sure that it is communicated and explained to staff throughout the firm and that a copy is posted in a prominent position in the waiting room
- recognise that although a first draft can be prepared by one person, the creation of one that is truly worthwhile can only be done as the result of a detailed discussion of values and aspirations.

Putting these guidelines into practice involves focusing upon two inter-related dimensions: the *client related issues* (what clients' needs do we intend meeting and where?); and the *key values* (what central or core

Figure 7.6 Mission statements

Sainsbury has stated its mission as being:

To discharge the responsibility as leaders in our trade by acting with complete integrity, by carrying out our work to the highest standards, and by contributing to the public good and to the quality of life in the community.

To provide unrivalled value to our customers in the quality of the goods we sell, in the competitiveness of our prices and in the choice we offer.

In our stores, to achieve the highest standards of cleanliness and hygiene, efficiency of operation, convenience and customer service, and thereby create as attractive and friendly a shopping environment as possible.

To offer our staff outstanding opportunities in terms of personal career development and in remuneration relative to other companies in the same market, practising always a concern for the welfare of every individual.

To generate sufficient profit to finance continual improvement and growth of the business whilst providing our shareholders with an excellent return on their investment.

Marks and Spencer's mission is broadly similar:

To offer our customers a selective range of high quality well designed and attractive merchandise at reasonable prices.

To encourage our suppliers to use the most modern and efficient techniques of production and quality control dictated by the latest discoveries in science and technology.

With the co-operation of our suppliers, to ensure the highest standards of quality control.

To plan the expansion of our stores for the better display of a widening range of goods (and) for the convenience of our customers.

To simplify operating procedures so that our business is carried on in the most efficient manner.

To foster good human relations with customers, suppliers and staff.

Planning for success (part 2): developing the marketing plan

values such as quality and levels of client service will it encompass and which we are simply not prepared to compromise on?), both of which are encompassed in the following mission statement:

> "As a firm, our mission is to provide our clients with the highest levels of legal care at all times by understanding, anticipating and responding to their full range of legal needs, providing a highly accessible service that is of the very highest quality that we are able to provide."

This statement incorporates a number of the guidelines that we highlighted earlier and whilst scope exists for some improvement, it has so far proved to be of enormous value within the firm in question in that it has highlighted the sorts of values that are seen to be at the heart of that firm.

Against the background of these comments, consider the following questions:
- Does your firm have a mission statement currently? If so, does it reflect the sorts of guidelines that we referred to earlier and incorporate the values that *really* are at the heart of the firm, or is it simply empty rhetoric?
- If the firm does not yet have a mission statement, what value do you think might be gained from developing one?

STEP TWO

Where do we want to go? How to set worthwhile objectives

To be effective, a planning system must be goal driven. The setting of clear and meaningful objectives is therefore a key step in the marketing planning process, since unless it is carried out effectively, everything that follows will lack focus and cohesion. The purpose of setting objectives is therefore to provide the firm with a sense of direction. In addition, however, they can be used as a basis for motivation as well as a benchmark against which performance and effectiveness can subsequently be measured.

The ten guidelines for setting worthwhile and meaningful objectives are straightforward and illustrated in figure 7.7.

Against the background of these guidelines, consider the following questions:
- What are the firm's short term and long term objectives currently?
- To what extent do the firm's objectives conform to the ten guidelines in figure 7.7?

- How often are the objectives reviewed in detail?
- How often and in what detail is performance against objectives measured?
- How much detailed thought is given to the process of developing and implementing the actions needed to achieve these objectives?

Figure 7.7 The ten guidelines for worthwhile objectives

Objectives need to be:

1 Hierarchial going from the most important to the least important

2 Quantifiable so that performance against target can be measured at a later stage

3 Limited in number. If you set a large number of objectives, it is likely that not only will you lose sight of at least some of them, but that you will make the process of developing a strategy capable of achieving all of them unnecessarily difficult. You should therefore concentrate upon identifying the most important areas in which objectives need to be set and then use these as the basis for developing the strategy

4 Realistic and a true reflection of the firm's strengths, the environmental opportunities, your contractual obligations, and the level of the firm's capability rather than a series of wishful thoughts

5 Consistent rather than mutually incompatible

6 Related to well-defined time periods

7 Stated explicitly with no scope for ambiguity

8 Based upon the firm's strengths and designed to help overcome weaknesses

9 Communicated to staff throughout the firm, with the implications for how they operate being explained to them

10 A reflection of the various elements of your mission statement.

Identifying the areas that your objectives should cover

In setting the objectives for the firm, you need to aim for a balance between several areas including:
- the partners' expectations;
- regulatory constraints;
- the expectations and needs of staff;
- the issues associated with the long term development of the firm, its premises and equipment; and
- clients' expectations of the quality and levels of service they will receive.

Although this is not an exhaustive list, it provides a useful framework for identifying the sorts of objectives that you might need to consider developing. Taking each of these in turn, you should therefore list the key points which need to be considered. In the case of clients, for example, you might identify issues such as how quickly they can get an appointment, the length of the interview, how long it takes to deal with correspondence or return telephone calls and so on. Under the heading of regulatory constraints you might include the achievement of full compliance with the Practice Management Standards and the attainment of a franchising contract, whilst staff related issues might include the attainment of Investors in People, levels of training and so on. Having identified the key issues under each of these and any other headings that you see to be important, you can then begin the process of refining the list of objectives, making them more specific, and attaching timescales so that some will be essentially short term (all reception staff to have reached a pre-determined level of information technology capability within twelve months), whilst others such as the complete refurbishment of the firm's premises will be longer term.

Having done this, you are then in a position to begin reviewing the objectives with a view to seeing which, if any, are unrealistic perhaps because of their magnitude (in other words, they are simply too ambitious) or because they are unlikely to be achieved in the short term but can be achieved over a slightly longer period. In doing this, you are trying to identify the nature and significance of any gaps that exist between the partners' expectations and the ability of partners and staff throughout the firm to meet these expectations. With this information, you can then either modify the objective or increase the degree of attention and the resources devoted to its achievement.

As an example of gap analysis, consider the objective of increasing revenue from commercial clients by 300 per cent over the next three years. By giving detailed thought to what is likely to be involved in achieving this, it may become apparent that it can be achieved only by recruiting more staff, opening a new office, making substantial changes to administrative procedures, and the development of a more proactive management/client seeking culture.

Having considered these implications, you may then decide that whilst the objective is laudable, the firm is simply not willing to make the sorts of changes that would be needed for it to be achieved. If this is the case, you need to go back and either modify the objective by watering it down or cross it out altogether. It may, of course, be at this stage that significant differences of opinion emerge as to the future of the firm. You may feel, for example, that you have developed a shared vision of the future but the realisation of what is actually needed to put it into effect may highlight fundamental differences of opinion. This is one of the benefits of a rigorous planning process, since it is far better to realise that such differences exist before embarking upon implementation. You must then either modify your vision and mission statement or even decide (hopefully amicably at this stage) to go separate ways. If such fundamental differences do exist, it is pointless to ignore them and early remedial action is always the best option to pursue.

STEP THREE

How are we going to get there? Developing action plans that will work

Having identified your short and long term objectives, you are then in a position to begin developing action plans. In doing this, you often need to be very specific and to pay considerable attention not just to the question of what needs to be done, but also to who is to be responsible for each element and what intermediate measures or checks of performance are needed; a framework for this appears in figure 7.8.

Once you have done this, you need to recognise that implementation is often the most difficult part of the planning process, since it is all too easy to be side-tracked by the sheer pressure of day-to-day activities. In the light of this, give thought to three questions:

1 Who within the firm is to be responsible for driving the plan?
2 How often do you intend holding review meetings to check on the progress being made and whether any corrective action is needed?
3 What sort of feedback are you going to give the staff on how well or badly the plan's implementation is proving to be?

Figure 7.8 The action planning framework

Objectives	Actions needed to achieve these objectives	Allocation of responsibilities	Intermediate performance measures
Short term • • • • **Long term** • • • •			

The question of who is to drive the plan is important, since whoever takes on the responsibility for this has to recognise from the outset that much of the plan's subsequent success will depend upon how well the job is done. It is therefore essential that in deciding who is to do this, that:
- they are fully committed to the plan and understand each of its elements in detail; and
- they have the authority and enthusiasm to make sure that no one loses sight of what the plan involves and what their contribution to its implementation should be.

How long should the plan be?

Perhaps the most frequently asked question that we have been faced with in discussing marketing plans with professional practices concerns the plan's length. Our advice is always the same: keep the plan as straightforward, short and simple as possible and, above all, make sure that it is capable of being used as a *working document*. Secondly, having written it, do not make the mistake of filing it or assuming that its implementation will take place as if by magic. The answer to the question of length is therefore a little difficult in that it is impossible to say whether it should be ten pages or twenty. Instead, we would remind you again of the benefits of the planning process (assuming, of course, that it has been done properly) in that it forces you to look not just at the detail of the firm's strengths and weaknesses, but also at the environment and the objectives that you intend pursuing. We would also highlight the way in which planning can clarify a considerable number of issues by bringing them into sharper focus and, again assuming that it has been done properly, lead to better patterns of communication, understanding and commitment throughout the firm. Having said all of this, the answer to the question of length has to be that it is not particularly important, but that the two overriding characteristics of worthwhile plans are, first, that they are used as working documents and reflect a planning culture in which full recognition is given to the benefits of the various stages of the analysis and so on, and second, that it helps you to achieve objectives that are seen within the firm to be worthwhile.

The nine planning pitfalls to avoid

In working with a variety of professional firms and helping the partners to develop marketing plans, we have encountered a number of common planning difficulties which, once you are aware of them, are relatively easy to overcome. They are:

1. A tendency to assume that budgeting and planning are one and the same thing; they are not.
2. The development of too many and unrealistically ambitious objectives.
3. An unclear vision of the sort of firm that the partners are trying to develop.
4. An emphasis upon analysis rather than decisions and implementation.
5. Poor internal communications with the result that levels of staff understanding and commitment to the plan are less than they should be.
6. Seeing planning as a ritual rather than an activity which is capable of making a real contribution to the development of the firm.
7. Inadequate resourcing and poor implementation procedures.
8. Failing to allocate responsibilities sufficiently.
9. Poor monitoring, feedback and control.

Against the background of our comments so far, it should be apparent that there is a set of simple guidelines for effective planning. These include the need to:
- Treat the plan as a working document (do not file it)
- Make it realistic and based on the firm's real strengths and weaknesses
- Keep it simple and user friendly
- Make sure that it reflects opportunities and comes to terms with any threats that exist or seem likely to emerge
- Ensure that it reflects a long term vision of the sort of firm you are trying to create
- Make sure that it improves teamworking and commitment
- See it as an opportunity to question the conventional wisdom
- Allocate responsibilities clearly
- Make sure the timescales are realistic
- Monitor performance and do not be afraid to take corrective action where it is needed
- Emphasise communication by getting others involved from the outset – osmosis is only rarely a useful or adequate method of communication
- Make sure that the plan can be and is implemented.

SUMMARY

Within this chapter we have focused upon the three principal steps of the planning process. Insofar as it is possible to identify the element that characterises effective planning, it would have to be the involvement and commitment of staff at all levels of the firm both to the development and to the implementation of the plan. Without this, any attempt at planning is likely to prove to be of little real value. Recognising this, there are three final guidelines which you need to bear in mind:
1. Avoid the ivory tower syndrome in which the senior partner develops the plan in isolation, presents it to other partners and staff, and then expects a full blooded commitment to its implementation.
2. Make sure that staff throughout the firm are involved in the process from as early a stage as possible and are then made fully aware of the contribution that is expected of them in its implementation.
3. Always provide feedback on how well or how badly the firm is performing, highlighting what the next stage of development will be.

CHAPTER 8

Using the marketing audit and the marketing effectiveness review to assess the true level of the firm's capability: revisiting your strengths and weaknesses

> Having read this chapter, you should:
> - understand the nature and role of the marketing audit;
> - be aware of the audit's components; and
> - understand how to conduct a marketing audit.

One of the biggest and most common problems faced by organisations, regardless of their type and size, is that plans all too often simply fail to come to fruition. There are several explanations for this, the most common of which are that the objectives set are too ambitious, too little thought is given to the activities needed to achieve the plan, and, faced with day to day pressures, staff lose sight of what they are trying to achieve. Because of this, and as we pointed out in Chapter 7, effective marketing planning must be based upon a clear statement of realistic objectives and a detailed understanding of what the firm is really capable of achieving. Although there are several ways in which the firm's capability can be measured, one of the most useful and straightforward tools for this is the marketing audit which requires you to focus upon a series of dimensions, such as the firm's strategy, its systems, the levels of productivity, and so on, with a view to identifying the real detail of the firm's strengths and weaknesses. The audit can then be taken a step further by conducting a review of marketing effectiveness (a framework for this appears in figure 8.3 at the end of the chapter).

Although the idea of looking at the firm's strengths, weaknesses, opportunities and threats was raised in chapters five and seven, our experience has shown that professionals often produce better and more tightly focused SWOT analyses if they are faced with a framework of questions rather than having to generate them themselves. It is this which, therefore, represents the real rationale for this chapter.

THE COMPONENTS OF THE AUDIT

The marketing audit involves looking in detail at six areas:
1 *The environment:* how are environmental forces developing currently and how are they likely to change in the short and the long term?
2 *The firm's strategy:* how well formulated are the objectives and the strategy and how well suited are they to the current and future environments?
3 *The organisation:* how capable is the firm of implementing any action plans that are developed?
4 *The systems:* how appropriate and effective are the firm's systems for planning and control?
5 *Productivity:* how cost effective are the different areas of the firm?
6 *Facilities and resources:* how well suited are the firm's facilities to what you are trying to achieve?

Quite deliberately, the audit that we discuss here is not all embracing, but is instead designed to encourage you to think about specific aspects of the firm. Supplementary questions can therefore be added to make it more directly relevant to an individual firm. In working your way through the six sections, you should therefore continually pose two fundamental questions:
- What are the implications of my answer for the firm?
- What are we/am I going to do about these implications?

For the results of the audit to be worthwhile, a few simple rules need to be kept in mind, including:
1 The process must be comprehensive and cover all parts of the firm rather than just a few known trouble spots;
2 It must be systematic and follow an orderly sequence of steps; and
3 It must be independent and not influenced by personal feelings, relationships or pre-conceived notions.

WHO SHOULD CONDUCT THE AUDIT?

With regard to who should conduct the audit, there are several possibilities. The first of these, which is also the cheapest and often the fastest, involves the practice manager or office manager taking on the responsibility. There are, however, potential disadvantages in this in that, with the best will in the world, he or she may not necessarily be totally objective. Because of this, within a number of the firms that we have dealt with, we have established a small audit task force consisting of the practice or office manager, one of the partners, and one or two other staff. By doing this, awkward questions are more likely to be addressed and a generally broader perspective brought to the exercise.

As you complete each section of the audit, you need to assess the implications of your answers with a view then to identifying the sorts of actions and responses that these demand of the firm; the framework for this is illustrated in figure 8.1, which appears towards the end of the chapter. As an example of this, if the strategy audit suggests that the firm's objectives are either not clearly stated or sufficiently well communicated to the staff throughout the firm, the steps to correct this need to be spelled out, responsibilities allocated, acted upon and a reporting back date agreed. Equally, if the productivity audit suggests that certain areas have cost levels that are too high, again an action plan to deal with this needs to be developed.

Having completed all six sections of the audit and conducted the marketing effectiveness review, the findings can then be pulled together in the form of the sort of SWOT (Strengths, Weaknesses, Opportunities and Threats) framework that we discussed initially in Chapter 5 and then in greater detail in Chapter 7, with thought being given to the actions needed to exploit strengths, convert any weaknesses to strengths, and threats to possible opportunities (refer back to figure 7.4).

COMPLETING THE MARKETING AUDIT

The environmental audit

- What effect will forecasted trends in the size, age distribution and regional distribution of the population have on the firm? For example, the Law Society has produced a forecast suggesting that the number of elderly clients with money to invest and property to dispose of will increase over the next few decades. Both this forecast and the Law Society's own SWOT analysis for the profession can be

found in 'Succeeding in the 90s'. In the case of commercial clients, what levels of activity seem likely?.
- What changes in attitude are taking place amongst the public towards legal firms?
- What changes are taking place in consumers' lifestyles and values that will have a bearing on our client groups?
- How do our current clients perceive and rate the firm?
- In what ways are our clients' expectations changing?
- What new services are likely to be required over the next few years?
- To what extent are our clients' current expectations being met?
- How might clients best be categorised (*e.g.* young/old, private/legal aid or private/commercial clients?) What are the expected rates of growth of each of these categories?
- How are other firms nearby perceived?
- How do other firms operate and what might we learn from them?
- How do different groups of clients appear to make their choice of solicitor and firm?
- How are the expectations of stakeholders likely to change over the next few years?

The strategy audit

- Are the firm's short term and long term objectives sufficiently clearly stated?
- Are they understood by everyone in the firm?
- Is there general agreement on their validity?
- Do the objectives provide sufficient guidance for planning and control purposes?
- Are the objectives appropriate given the demands of clients and the external environment?
- Is there a well-formulated overall strategy?
- If so, are staff aware of the strategy and the nature of the contribution that they are expected to make to it?
- Have sufficient resources been made available for the objectives to be achieved?
- Have the resources been optimally allocated across the various client groups?
- Are there any new services that we might offer?
- Are there any existing services that we might offer to new client groups?
- Are there any services that might benefit from minor or major changes being made to them?

- Are there any services that we offer currently which should be dropped?
- Is there any scope for offering more of our existing services to our existing clients?
- What are the firm's promotional objectives?
- Is there a well-conceived publicity programme and does it comply with the Publicity Code?

The organisational audit

- Is there someone who has direct responsibility for planning and monitoring performance? If so, does this person have adequate authority?
- Are responsibilities within the firm clearly spelled out and understood?
- Are the lines of communication and working relations between staff operating as effectively as they might?
- Are lines of authority within the firm clearly spelled out?
- Is there any scope for more delegation of routine tasks to support staff?
- Are there any individuals within the firm who need more training, motivation, supervision or evaluation?
- Have admitted staff undergone all the relevant training including CPD?
- Do staff evaluations take place regularly? Is there evidence that they are effective?
- Is there sufficient teamworking particularly between fee earners and secretaries?
- What conflicts exist within the firm?
- Do you hold regular brainstorming sessions in order to identify how levels of client service might be improved?
- Is the task of motivation taken sufficiently seriously or is it assumed that all staff will always be well motivated?
- Are briefing and feedback sessions held on a regular basis?
- Is an open managerial style in operation?
- Do you have effective partners' meetings? Is there a proper agenda agreed and distributed in advance so that the meeting is both efficient and effective?

The systems audit

- Has the firm fully considered the possible benefits of adopting the Law Society Practice Management Standards, Legal Aid Franchising, Investors in People and/or a recognised quality system such as BS EN ISO 9000?

- Is the system for identifying the significant happenings outside the firm working effectively?
- Is the planning system well conceived and effective?
- Are realistic targets set for staff?
- Is there an adequate monitoring system in place so that performance is measured objectively?
- Are the control procedures (monthly and quarterly) to ensure that the annual plan objectives are met operating effectively?
- Is sufficient provision made to monitor, analyse and evaluate the costs of various services?
- Is the firm organised to ensure that new ideas are generated and evaluated?
- What mechanisms exist to ensure that levels of client satisfaction are being monitored?
- Is there a complaints procedure in place and are complaints regularly reviewed to detect trends and take appropriate action?
- Have the other requirements of Practice Rule 15 been introduced and are they working effectively?
- Is there someone who has direct responsibility for compliance with the Practice Rules and Law Society requirements and does that person have adequate authority?
- Are the computer systems working effectively and are they adequate for the ways in which the firm will probably develop?
- Are the provisions of the Accounts Rules being followed and are regular bank reconciliations taking place?

The productivity audit

- What formal mechanisms exist to ensure that all cost areas are reviewed on a regular basis?
- Do any activities appear to have excessive costs?
- What steps are being taken to:
  (i) control costs
  (ii) reduce costs?
- Are brainstorming sessions held on a regular basis in order to identify how levels of productivity might possibly be improved?
- Do there appear to be any unnecessary procedures or processes within the firm?
- Are there any procedures or processes that might usefully be modified?

The facilities and resources audit

- How do clients view our premises?
- What changes do we need to make to improve them?

- Is the firm adequately resourced to achieve the objectives that have been set?
- In which areas is further investment needed?
- What obstacles do clients experience in visiting us?

Having conducted the audit, there are several questions which need to be considered:
- what picture of the firm emerges?
- what areas within the firm do we need to pay attention to in the short term and in the long term?
- what courses of action do we need to take?
- who is to be given the responsibility for each of these?
- what are the resource implications of any changes that are needed?

One further question that needs to be raised concerns the issue of cause and effect. Where something has gone wrong or levels of performance are not as high as they might or should be, you need to spend time identifying why this has happened and who is primarily responsible. In doing this, the purpose is not to point the finger of blame but is instead designed to highlight the nature of any training that might be needed to overcome a skills problem and/or whether a change in the allocation of responsibilities might be appropriate.

The audit findings can then be taken a step further by conducting a review of marketing effectiveness; the framework for this appears in figure 8.3.

The review involves focusing in turn, upon five areas: the client philosophy; the marketing organisation; marketing information, the strategic perspective; and operational efficiency. By working through each of these, an overall measure of effectiveness can be arrived at, with this then being extended by looking at each of the five sections with a view to identifying the area(s) in which the firm appears particularly weak.

SUMMARY

By completing the marketing audit and the review of the marketing effectiveness, you should have a far deeper understanding of the firm's marketing capabilities. This deeper understanding can then be applied to figure 8.2 which is designed as a simple framework to highlight those areas in need of attention.

Figure 8.1 The findings and implications of the marketing audit

Findings	The implications	Actions required
The environmental audit		
•		
•		
•		
•		
The strategy audit		
•		
•		
•		
•		
The organisational audit		
•		
•		
•		
•		
The systems audit		
•		
•		
•		
•		
The productivity audit		
•		
•		
•		
•		
The facilities and resources audit		
•		
•		
•		
•		

Figure 8.2 External, internal and interactive marketing

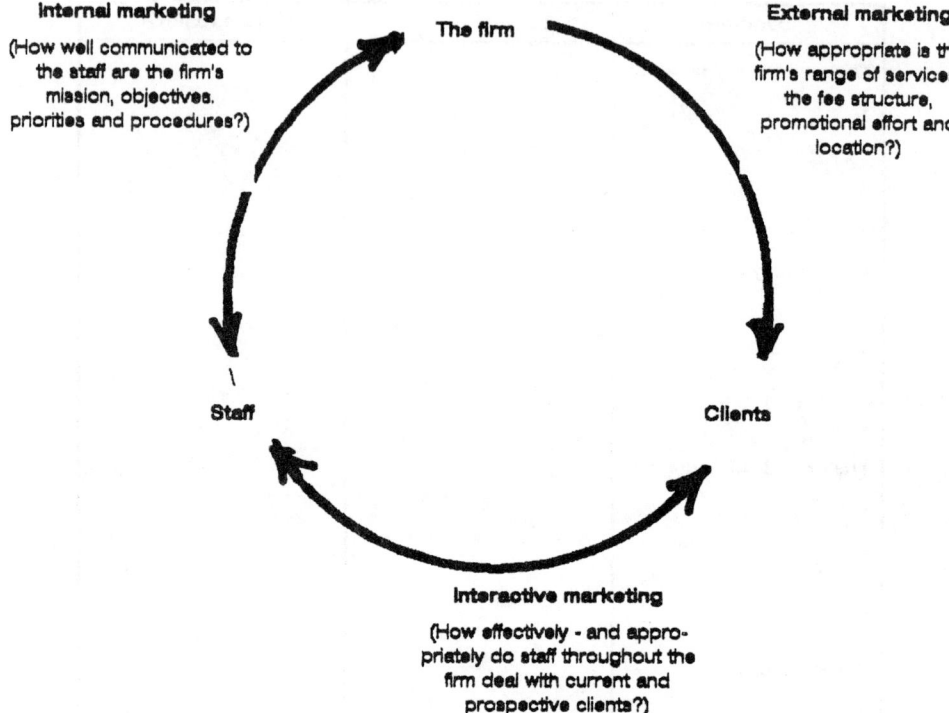

[External marketing is concerned especially with the 'hard' elements of the marketing mix, interactive marketing with the 'soft' elements.]

Beginning with the interface between the firm and its clients, consider the nature of the external marketing effort and, in particular, the appropriateness of the firm's range of services, the levels of expertise, issues of quality, the fee structures, the promotional effort and the location of the offices. Turn then to the interface between the firm and its staff and consider the nature and effectiveness of the internal marketing processes. How well communicated, for example, are the firm's objectives and priorities? Finally, turn to the staff-client interface and consider how well – or badly – this operates.

Taking these points together, what do they tell you about the firm and its areas of strength and weakness?

Figure 8.3 The marketing effectiveness review

Client philosophy

                                                                      Score

1 To what extent do the partners recognise the need to organise the firm to satisfy specific client and market demands?

    The practice philosophy is to sell existing and new services to whoever will buy them.   0 ☐

    The partners attempt to serve a wide range of markets and needs with equal effectiveness.   1 ☐

    Having identified market needs, the partners focus upon specific target markets in order to maximise the practice's growth and potential.   2 ☐

2 To what extent is the marketing programme tailored to the needs of different market segments?

    Not at all.   0 ☐

    To some extent.   1 ☐

    To a very high degree.   2 ☐

3 Do the partners adopt a systems approach to planning, with recognition being given to the interrelationships between the environment, suppliers, clients, and competitors?

    Not at all; the practice focuses solely upon its existing client base.   0 ☐

    To some extent, in that the majority of its effort goes into serving its immediate and existing client base.   1 ☐

    Yes. The partners recognise the various dimensions of the marketing environment and attempt to reflect this in the practice's marketing programme by taking account of the threats and opportunities created by change within the system.   2 ☐

(continued)

Marketing organisation

4 To what extent does the senior partner attempt to control and integrate the marketing effort?

    Not at all. No real attempt is made to integrate or control the various dimensions of the marketing programme, with the result that it is disorganised and lacks focus.   0 ☐

    To a limited degree, although the levels of control and coordination are generally unsatisfactory.   1 ☐

    To a very high degree with the result that the marketing effort works well.   2 ☐

5 What sort of relationship exists between the fee earners in each specialism and between the fee earners and the various support staff and/or departments?

    Generally poor, with frequent complaints being made that unrealistic demands are made.   0 ☐

    Generally satisfactory, although the feeling exists that each department (or individual) is intent on serving its own needs.   1 ☐

    Overall very good, with departments and individuals working together well in the interests of the firm as a whole.   2 ☐

6 How well organised is the process for the development of new services?

    Not very well at all.   0 ☐

    New services are developed but in a spasmodic way.   1 ☐

    New services are well researched, quickly developed and achieve good results.   2 ☐

(continued)

Marketing information

7 How frequently does the firm conduct market research studies of its clients and competitors?
    Seldom, if ever.   0 ☐
    Occasionally.   1 ☐
    Regularly and in a highly structured way.   2 ☐

8 To what extent are the partners aware of the potential and profitability of different market segments, clients and the various services offered?
    Not at all.   0 ☐
    To some degree.   1 ☐
    To a very high degree.   2 ☐

9 What effort is made to measure the cost effectiveness of different levels and types of marketing expenditure?
    None at all.   0 ☐
    Some, but not in a regular or structured way.   1 ☐
    A great deal.   2 ☐

The strategic perspective

10 How formalised is the marketing planning process?
    The firm does virtually no formal marketing planning.   0 ☐
    An annual marketing plan is developed.   1 ☐
    The firm develops a detailed annual marketing plan and a long-range plan that is updated annually.   2 ☐

(continued)

11 What is the quality of thinking that underlies the current marketing strategy?

    The current strategy is unclear.   0 ☐

    The current strategy is clear and is largely a continuation of earlier strategy.   1 ☐

    The current strategy is clear, well argued and well developed.   2 ☐

12 To what extent do the partners engage in contingency thinking and planning?

    Not at all.   0 ☐

    There is some contingency thinking but this is not incorporated into a formal planning process.   1 ☐

    A serious attempt is made to identify the most important contingencies, and contingency plans are then developed.   2 ☐

Operational efficiency

13 How well is the partners' thinking on marketing communicated and implemented down the line?

    Very badly.   0 ☐

    Reasonably well.   1 ☐

    Extremely successfully.   2 ☐

14 Do the partners do an effective marketing job with the resources available?

    No. The resource base is inadequate for the objectives that have been set.   0 ☐

    To a limited extent. The resources available are adequate but are only rarely applied in an optimal manner.   1 ☐

    Yes. The resources available are adequate and managed efficiently.   2 ☐

(continued)

15 Do the partners respond quickly and effectively to unexpected developments in the market-place?

    No. Market information is typically out of date and the partners' responses are slow.   0 ☐

    To a limited extent. Market information is reasonably up to date, although the partners' response times vary.   1 ☐

    Yes. Highly efficient information systems exist and the partners respond quickly and effectively.   2 ☐

The scoring process

Each solicitor works his way through the 15 questions in order to arrive at a score. The scores are then aggregated and averaged. The overall measure of marketing effectiveness can then be assessed against the following scale:

0-5	=	None	16-20	=	Good
6-10	=	Poor	21-25	=	Very good
11-15	=	Fair	26-30	=	Superior

With a score of 10 or less major questions can be asked about the firm's ability to survive in anything more than the short term, since any serious competitive challenge is likely to create significant problems. Fundamental changes are needed both in the partners' philosophy and the organisational structure. For many firms in this position, however, these changes are unlikely to be brought about by the existing partners, since it is this group which has led to the current situation. The solution may therefore lie in major changes to the management of the firm.

With a score of between 11 and 15 there is again a major opportunity to improve the firm's management philosophy and organisational structure.

With a score of between 16 and 25 scope for improvement exists, although this is likely to be in terms of a series of small changes and modifications rather than anything more fundamental. With a score of between 26 and 30, care needs to be taken to ensure that the proactive stance is maintained and that complacency does not begin to emerge.

Source: Adapted from Kotler P, (1991) Marketing Management: analysis, planning, implementation and control (Prentice Hall)

CHAPTER 9

Developing the firm's marketing mix

> Having read this chapter, you should:
> - understand the various elements that make up the marketing mix; and
> - have an appreciation of the nature and significance of the role played by the mix within the marketing process and of the ways in which managing the mix is capable of affecting the demand for the firm's services.

We first made reference to the marketing mix in Chapter 2, suggesting that it consists of seven dimensions – the product/service, promotion, place, price, people, process management and physical elements. Together, these elements, which are sometimes referred to as the 7Ps, make up the marketing toolkit that is used to shape the profile of the firm that is presented to the world.

Within this chapter we focus upon each of the seven elements in turn and then, against this background, discuss how they can be brought together in the form of a coherent marketing programme and action plan.

THE 'HARD' AND THE 'SOFT' ELEMENTS OF THE MIX

Although we typically refer to the mix in terms of the 7Ps, it is possible to divide the mix into two distinct parts – the 'hard' elements and the 'soft' elements. The hard elements consist of the product/service; the price/fee; the forms of promotion and the price/location in which the service is delivered. The soft elements then consist of the people who deliver the service (legal and support); the form of process management (how clients are dealt with from the very first to the very last form of contact); and the physical evidence (what do the waiting areas and offices look like and what images do they convey).

Because many clients, particularly non-commercial clients, buy legal services infrequently, they typically buy in a relatively unsophisticated way. Their assumption is therefore likely to be that, until proved wrong, the quality of the product (that is the legal advice) is high. They therefore tend to arrive at their perceptions of quality and value largely on the basis of the 'soft' factors, such as the reception staff, the waiting areas, the types of correspondence, and so on. It is for this reason that in marketing legal services particular care needs to be given to these areas.

THE MARKETING MIX

The product/service

Almost invariably, the starting point for any discussion of the marketing mix has to be the product or service offered, since it is this which provides the basis for virtually all other marketing decisions. In the case of law firms, the 'product' that clients receive is, of course, the professional service and advice given (refer to figure 3.1) and is made up of three distinct dimensions: the product's attributes, its benefits, and the nature of the support services; these are illustrated in figure 9.1.

- *service attributes* are associated with the core service itself and are made up of the various legal procedures
- *service benefits* are the various elements that clients perceive as meeting their needs – this is sometimes referred to as the 'bundle of satisfactions.' Included within this is the perceived and actual effectiveness of the advice given or work done and the reassurances that the client is given
- *the support services* consist of all the elements that the firm provides in addition to the core service. These would typically include the appointments system, the reception staff and their manner, how the telephones are answered and correspondence dealt with and the relationships that exist between the firm, the courts and other local professionals.

In looking at figure 9.1, there are several issues that emerge which are of potentially considerable significance. The first of these is the extent to which the support services are capable of setting the tone for any visit. Following on from this is the way in which product benefits are capable of being influenced not so much by the reality, but by the

Figure 9.1 The three levels of the product/service

Figure 9.2 Checking out your support services

The support services
- Is the firm's phone system capable of handling the volume of calls you receive or do clients often find themselves getting an engaged tone?
- Are all the reception staff sufficiently approachable, courteous, helpful and knowledgeable?
- Has the appointments system been designed for the convenience of clients or staff?
- Is there a general culture within the firm of getting things right first time and done on time?
- Are the firm's relationships with other professionals as satisfactory and well-developed as they might be?
- What sorts of problems have been encountered in the system of:
   (i) diary entries of future dates for action;
   (ii) retrieving clients' documents promptly; and
   (iii) archiving papers after completed transactions?
- What scope exists for changes and improvements for the client in each of these areas?

Service benefits: the bundle of satisfactions
- Do you have a detailed understanding of how clients perceive each of the solicitors within the firm?
- How do clients appear to perceive the firm in each of the following areas:
   (i) the advice given;
   (ii) the accurate preparation of documents;
   (iii) the explanation of what work is to be done;
   (iv) the level of fees charged;
   (v) the general efficiency of the firm;
   (vi) how up-to-date the firm is; and
   (vii) how quickly it gets on with the job?
- In what areas does there appear to be scope for improvements? What would be involved in making these improvements and what obstacles would be encountered?

The core service
- What range of services do you offer currently?
- What scope exists for developing each of these services?
- What scope exists for extending these services?
- Are there any services which are offered currently which, for one reason or another, you should consider dropping?

client's perceptions (it might be useful at this stage to refer again briefly to our discussion in Chapter 3 of what clients really want from their solicitors (this appears on page 33)). The third factor is that against this background, legal competence, levels of expertise and issues of quality are often taken for granted by clients and, in a client-centred firm in particular, are the areas which they are least likely to question.

Given the nature of these comments, you might usefully consider the questions which appear in figure 9.2.

In answering this final question, there are two models – the product life cycle and the Ansoff matrix – which are commonly used in marketing and which might be of help in structuring your thinking; these are illustrated in figures 9.3 and 9.4.

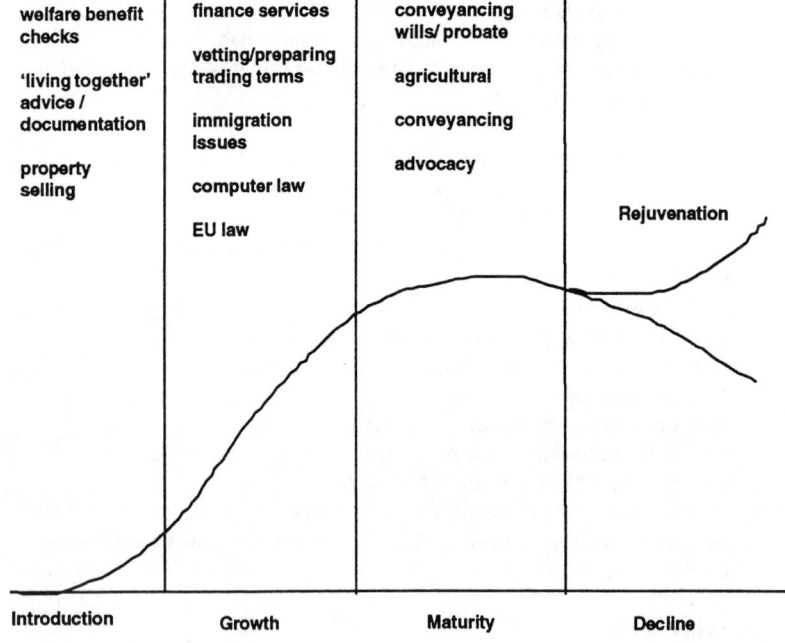

Figure 9.3 The product life cycle

The product life cycle is, in many ways, one of the best known and straightforward of marketing models, and based on the idea that any product or service has a finite life and that during this life there is a need to manage it in particular ways, depending upon the position it has reached.

The majority of the services offered by law firms are, by their very nature, likely to be in the mature phase. However, if the firm is to develop over the next few years and exploit the opportunities either that exist currently or which offer scope for development, you need to consider what additional services might be introduced or, in the case of some of the services offered currently, might be encouraged to grow.

To use the life cycle as a planning tool, you need therefore to begin by positioning each of your services on the curve. Having done this, take each of the services in turn and ask whether scope exists for its expansion and growth. If so, think about the sorts of actions that would be needed to do this and what degree of growth might be possible. In the case of financial services, for example, considerable opportunities undoubtedly exist for their development in many firms, although in order to realise this potential, a series of possibly significant investment steps and the development of a number of skills would be needed. By contrast, many firms could expand the number of wills they make relatively quickly and at a low cost simply by taking the opportunities that already exist. Many firms undertaking matrimonial work overlook the need to advise the client about willmaking. Quite apart from missing an opportunity, this is possibly negligent.

Where the demand for services appears to have stopped growing and has reached maturity, several possibilities exist. The first involves managing the service in such a way that it stays in profitable maturity almost indefinitely by ensuring, for example, that the amount of legal advice given remains constant and that levels of efficiency in this area are improved. An alternative approach would involve the decision to expand the firm by recruiting a new partner, opening a branch office, or merging with another firm. Above all, of course, you need to guard against the gradual decline of the firm either in absolute or relative terms as the result of a series of external changes such as the insolvency or shutdown of a major local employer or a housing redevelopment which leads to people moving away.

Having used the product life cycle as the first step, you need then to think about how the Ansoff matrix can contribute to planning. The matrix, which is illustrated in figure 9.4, involves looking initially at your existing services and markets with a view to identifying the scope that exists for:
1 extending existing products/services into new or untapped market sectors (*e.g.* promoting existing will making services to those clients who you rarely see);
2 developing new products/services for existing markets (*e.g.* introducing employment contract advice or drawing up new conditions of sale and promoting them to your existing clients);

3 developing new products/services for new or untapped markets (e.g. the development of a specialism such as intellectual property, media law or property selling).

Figure 9.4 The Ansoff matrix

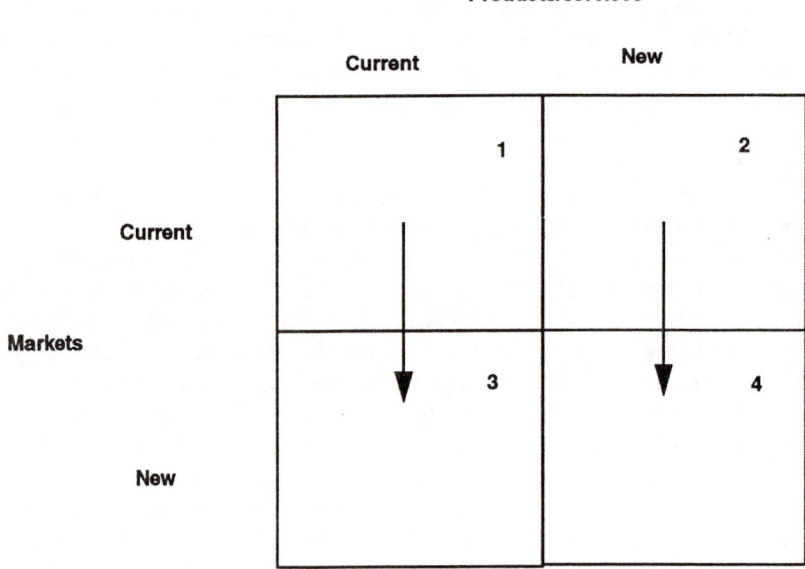

To use the matrix, begin by listing as many of your existing services in the top left hand cell of the matrix. Having done this, use brainstorming to generate as many ideas as possible of how all or some of these might be moved into cell two. Try then to identify a range of new services that might be developed and offered to your existing markets (cell three) and, in turn, how these might be extended into cell four.

Having generated these ideas, the next step involves assessing their viability by giving detailed thought to what would be involved in developing each service and market, whether this would prove to be cost-effective, and indeed whether this would be a development that, individually, the partners would welcome. In doing this, there is a further framework that can be of help; this is illustrated in figure 9.5 (a) and (b). To use the matrix in 9.5 (b), you need to begin by using the first column of the table in 9.5 (a) to list as many areas of client need as possible. Having done this, complete the second column which is concerned with the firm's ability/willingness to service effectively each of these areas of client need.

The next stage involves positioning each of these areas in the appropriate cells of the matrix in figure 9.5 (b). From the picture that emerges, you should then be in a position to identify those areas in which you might usefully concentrate some of the firm's future energies and those from which you might possibly either withdraw or at least reduce your focus. In the case of the *money makers,* for example, there is an obvious incentive to increase the firm's effort. With the *areas for consideration,* detailed thought needs to be given to the various ways in which the firm's efforts might possibly be channelled in these directions; the obvious area, of course, from which at least some of this resource might come is the *wasted effort* cell.

Equally, serious thought needs to be given to the future of those activities which appear in the *back drawer* cell.

Figure 9.5 (a) Client needs and the firm's ability to service the need

Areas of client need	Ability of the firm to service each area of client need
•	High/Low*
•	High/Low*
•	High/Low*
•	High/Low*
•	High/Low*
•	High/Low*
•	High/Low*
•	High/Low*
	*delete as applicable

Figure 9.5 (b) Clients' needs and the law firm match

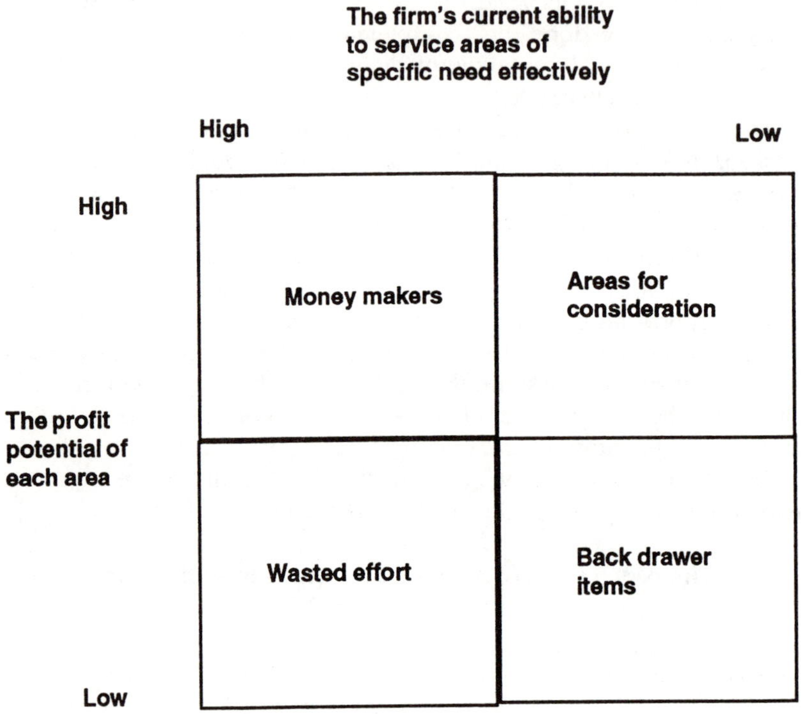

The firm's current ability to service areas of specific need effectively

	High	Low
High (profit potential)	Money makers	Areas for consideration
Low	Wasted effort	Back drawer items

The profit potential of each area

Promotion

Because solicitors are now allowed to advertise, there are several ways in which the firm can be promoted. However, before discussing some of the ways in which this might be done, you need to give thought to the sort of image that you would like to create for the firm. Is it, for example, that of a highly innovative, thrusting, dynamic and high technology partnership or one that is wedded to traditional values? The answer to this will depend in part upon the types of partners you have, but also upon the types of clients you deal with. In some instances, of course, clients might well be disconcerted by what they see to be an overly modern and aggressive approach in what has traditionally been a very conservative profession.

In thinking about how you will manage this part of the marketing mix, you should therefore begin by considering four questions:
1 What sort of image does the firm have currently?
2 What sort of image do you, as solicitors, want to create?
3 What sort of image do your clients want and what will they feel most comfortable with?
4 What sorts of images do other firms locally have?

Having done this, think about the wide variety of ways in which clients build up an image of the firm. Typically this includes the age and manner of the solicitors, the type and location of the premises, the ways in which the telephone is answered, the reception staff, the waiting area, the fee earners' rooms, the look of the office equipment, letters and letter headings, word of mouth, the solicitors' cars, and so on.

Recognition of this should give you a better understanding of the number of areas to which you will have to pay attention if you do decide to make any real change to the image that exists currently. In some cases, of course, some of the areas that we have identified can be changed at relatively low cost; the firm's leaflets and the letter headings are obvious examples. In other cases, however, changes will either be far more difficult, time-consuming and expensive, or simply not open to modification; the age and manner of solicitors tend to spring to mind as the most obvious examples of the sorts of constraints which you would have to work around.

It should be apparent from these comments that there is probably very little that can be gained from playing around with just one or two promotional elements, and that a far more focused effort is likely to be needed. Figure 9.6 should help in achieving this.

Against the background of your answers to these questions, spend some time thinking about the complete spectrum of factors that contribute to the firm's image; in addition to those that we identified at an earlier stage in this section, there may be:
- publicity in local newspapers;
- the firm's leaflets and brochures;
- the firm's newsletters;
- the entry in the Yellow Pages and other directories; and
- letters to clients (not just the letter heads and style of the letter, but also the type of paper and envelopes).

In each case, try to be objective by standing to one side and asking yourself what you would think of each of these if you were looking at them for the first time. Having done this, consider how each one might be improved (never be afraid to look at what other solicitors and other professionals such as doctors, accountants, surveyors and so on are doing, with a view to learning from them).

> **Figure 9.6 The promotion check-up checklist**
>
> - What overall image does the firm have currently?
>
> - What image do you want to create?
>
> - How big a shift is going to be required in order to achieve this?
>
> - In what ways might each of the promotional elements contribute to this new image?
>
> - How big is the promotional budget for the next 12 months?
>
> - Who will have the responsibility for developing and implementing the new image?
>
> - What design skills do you have within the firm? (Never forget that highly developed design skills are relatively rare and that you will probably save a lot of time and effort by going to a design shop at the outset rather than trying to do it yourself or letting one of the reception staff do it 'because she's creative').

Try also a brainstorming session. What scope exists, for example, for:
- using the records system for completed cases or wills and deeds to target certain groups of clients *with a personal letter* to tell them about a particularly relevant service?
- running a question and answer column in the local newspaper or a legal trivia quiz at Christmas?

Having gone through this exercise, concentrate upon developing the action plan that will help to achieve and reinforce the image that you are trying to create. In doing this, never lose sight of three golden rules:
- have a clear 'house style' which is used on all forms of promotion;
- keep messages simple; and
- always emphasise the benefits that clients will receive.

With these in mind, you can then move on to the sort of action plan that appears in figure 9.7.

Figure 9.7 The promotion action plan

The image that we want to create is that of a firm which is................ .... The ways in which we will do this will include:			
	Key messages	Timing	Responsibility
• The firm's leaflets and brochures • Yellow pages and other directories • Publicity in local newspapers • Letters to the clients • Notices in the waiting room • The firm's newsletter • What staff tell clients • The layout and decor of the waiting room			

Place and the physical elements

For our purposes here, the place and physical elements of the firm's marketing mix can be discussed in tandem, since they are concerned with three interrelated factors:
- the location of the firm;
- its accessibility; and
- its general ambience and the sorts of messages that clients receive from it both internally and externally.

In evaluating this part of the mix, you should therefore give consideration to several questions, including:

1. How conveniently is it located? (Although in the short term you might not be able to change the location, there is almost certain to be scope in the longer term).
2. Are any branch offices needed?
3. How accessible does the appointments system make the firm?
4. How often does the appointments system run late (and how may clients are affected)?

5 What does the design, layout, cleanliness and warmth of the waiting room say about the firm?
6 Are there sufficient distractions for clients while they are waiting? Examples of these would include newspapers, topical and up-to-date magazines but no clock (if you are running late there is no point in providing a constant reminder for the client).
7 How does it compare with the waiting rooms of other professionals such as doctors, estate agents and accountants?
8 Would you feel comfortable sitting in the waiting room as it is laid out currently?
9 Can you put together an album of promotional material such as cuttings from any good press coverage so that new clients can be quietly impressed reading it whilst they are waiting?
10 Do you instruct staff to offer drinks of coffee or tea to clients as a matter of course?

Price

In any discussion of the firm's marketing mix, price often proves to be the most difficult to come to terms with. For some clients price is relatively unimportant, such as when the costs are covered by legal expenses insurance or when an employer is covering the costs of a house move under a relocation scheme. However, price is important for the majority of clients, even for those receiving legal aid since the certificate may be discharged or revoked. Clients are increasingly questioning the level of charges, with corporate clients in many cases now being willing to shop around for competitive charges. However, it is not necessarily the cheapest firms which will attract the work: clients typically seek value for money and so if additional benefits are offered and perceived, then premium prices are more likely to be paid. Nevertheless, for work that can be done by competitors outside the profession, there may be a difficulty in competing on cost alone, since solicitors face a higher level of regulation than most organisations and this increases the base cost of doing the work. In looking at the price element of the mix, it is perhaps easier therefore to focus upon issues of cost and in particular just how cost effective each element of the firm is. Given this, think about the question of:

- How detailed is our understanding of the costs of each major dimension of the firm?
- Are there any areas in which costs are unnecessarily high?
- In what ways and in what areas might we be more cost effective?
- What scope exists for selling a *package* of services?

People

In our earlier discussion of the product/service component of the mix, we highlighted the significance of client perception and how this is influenced by the manner, behaviour and responses not just of the solicitor, but also of the reception and other support staff. Because of this, the effective management of the people element of the mix has to be seen as a crucial part of the firm's marketing effort, since it is capable of making or breaking the marketing programme. Consider therefore, the following questions:

Support staff
- How rigorous is your selection procedure for support staff?
- What initial and subsequent training do they receive?
- Are the staff encouraged to work in teams and do these teams work effectively?
- Do you encourage or demand a certain standard of dress? Do you have a uniform that staff are required to wear?
- What effort has gone into client care training?
- What problems do you appear to have amongst your support staff?
- What are working relationships like?
- Are there sufficient support staff of the right sort and with the right skills to enable you to achieve the firm's objectives?

Fee earners
- Are the fee earners fully up-to-date with legal and administrative procedures?
- Have they been properly trained in how to handle clients effectively or do they just rely upon common sense? (Never forget that common sense is an all too rare commodity)
- What additional training will they require over the next few years?
- Are working relationships between the fee earners satisfactory?
- Are the working relationships between the fee earners and the support staff as effective as they might be?

Looking at the firm overall:
- Do you have the right blend of skills and experience for what is being demanded of law firms in the mid to late 1990s?
- What are levels of motivation and morale like?

In the light of your answers to these questions, you should be in a better position to begin the process of identifying in greater detail the sorts of skills and knowledge gaps that exist and which are likely to affect the client experience and hence their perceptions of the firm.

Process management

The final part of the mix is concerned with the ways in which clients and information are handled. Although we have already made a number of references to issues such as how clients are handled both by the reception/support staff and the fee earners, it is worth posing just a few more questions. How, for example, are clients addressed? Is it in a relatively formal way or, as we came across in one firm, as 'Luv' or 'Duck' and on one memorable occasion, as 'Mate'? How are clients summoned by the solicitor? Is it by the solicitor shouting down the corridor 'Next!', or is it by a member of the reception staff? Do the members of the reception staff point the client vaguely in the direction of the solicitor's office or do they always take each client to the door of the office and introduce them by name? Whichever approach is used, think clearly about how you would feel if you were the client in these circumstances.

The second dimension of process management is concerned with the ways in which the various systems within the firm operate, including the clients' filing systems, and the accuracy of the relevant recording process. The questions that you should therefore consider under this heading include:
- Are we making as much use of information technology as we might or should?
- How might the various systems be developed?
- What information do we need to make the firm work more effectively and deliver a higher level of client service?
- Do we have a clear idea of how we might do this?

DEVELOPING THE ACTION PLAN

Having looked at each of the individual elements of the marketing mix, you need to begin the process of pulling them together in the form of an action plan; a framework to help with this appears in figure 9.8. To complete the framework, start by identifying your objectives under each of the six headings (remember that although we refer to the 7Ps of the marketing mix, for the purposes of our discussion here we amalgamated the place and physical elements). Then move on to list in as much detail as possible the action steps that will need to be taken in order to achieve the objectives. However, recognising that not every objective or action is of equal importance or equally pressing, try then to assess the degree of priority and the timescales over which the various

Developing the firm's marketing mix 123

courses of action should take place. From here, move on to identify the broad levels of costs that will be incurred and then, finally, begin the process of allocating responsibilities.

Figure 9.8 The marketing mix action planning framework

	Objectives	Summary of the actions needed to achieve the objectives	Degree of priority	Timescales	Costs	Responsibility
Product/ service						
Promotion						
Place/ physical elements						
Price						
People						
Process Management						

FOCUSING THE MARKETING EFFORT

As in life generally, so it is that in marketing it is only rarely possible to be all things to all people. Because of this, any marketing programme for the firm needs to reflect the needs and expectations of each of the different types of client that you are dealing with currently or intend focusing your marketing effort upon in the future. There are various ways in which existing and prospective clients can be categorised, the most obvious of which is in terms of private versus commercial. However, within each of these a variety of other dimensions exist, some of which are illustrated in figure 9.9. In marketing terms this categorisation is referred to as market segmentation, targeting and positioning (see figure 9.10).

Figure 9.9 The bases for client segmentation

Commercial clients	Client characteristics	Private clients
Low → medium → high	Size/importance of the client	Low → medium
Low → medium → high	Scope for long term development and fee potential	Low → medium
Occasional → regular	Frequency with which legal advice is needed/requested	One off, regular, frequent
Unsophisticated/sophisticated	Expectations of the firm	Unsophisticated/sophisticated
Commercial conveyancing, intellectual property, media law, acquisitions company formation	Nature of client needs and benefits sought	Matrimonial, conveyancing, probate, accident, financial advice, criminal, litigation
Low → high	Sophistication/complexity of client needs	Low → high
Local/national/regional/international	Geographic location	Local
Long established exclusive use/single specific transactions	Loyalty to the firm/use of other firms	Long established exclusive use, single specific transactions
Client, third party	Source of payment	Client, third party, Legal Aid, legal expense insurance
Retainer plus fee/fee only	Basis of payment	Fee only
Low → high	Fee sensitivity	Low → high
Low → high	Importance of personal relationships	Low → high

The thinking behind what is sometimes labelled STP marketing is straightforward and can be expressed most readily in terms of the fact that because the needs, wants and expectations of clients differ – sometimes significantly – any worthwhile marketing programme needs to be based upon a recognition of these differences, with these differences then being reflected either in the nature of the product/service that is offered and/or in the way in which it is offered.

In terms of *how* this might be done, begin by using figure 9.10 to develop a picture of the market and the most meaningful bases for market segmentation. Having done this, identify those segments which you feel offer the greatest potential for your firm. To do this, you need to think about the extent to which the firm's capabilities and specialisms match the needs and expectations of each of the segments that have been identified. The third step involves deciding upon the positioning strategy which you intend adopting in each of the segments (positioning, in these circumstances relates to your general strategic and competitive stance and, in particular, to the question of the sorts of services and values for which you want the firm to be known; this is illustrated in figure 9.11).

In identifying the various bases for segmentation that appear in figure 9.9 we are not arguing that all of these approaches should be used, but rather that you should go through the list identifying those that are most relevant to your firm. Having done this, you can then begin thinking about how any marketing effort might more precisely reflect the specifics of each of the target groups. As an example of this, you might decide that the age profile of the firm's private clients is too high and that an effort to attract a greater number of younger clients with a greater diversity of legal needs and offering a greater long term potential is needed. You might then focus upon the sort of approach and positioning stance that would be required to make the firm appeal to these groups. Equally, in the case of commercial work, think about areas of specialism, the sophistication/complexity of client needs, the long term fee potential, the nature of client expectations, the frequency with which legal advice will be needed, and so on.

Given the nature of these comments, consider the following questions:
- In what ways might current and prospective clients be most effectively segmented?
- How do the needs, wants and expectations of each of these segments differ?
- To what extent do the firm's capabilities match the needs and expectations of each of these segments?

Figure 9.10 The segmentation, targeting and positioning process

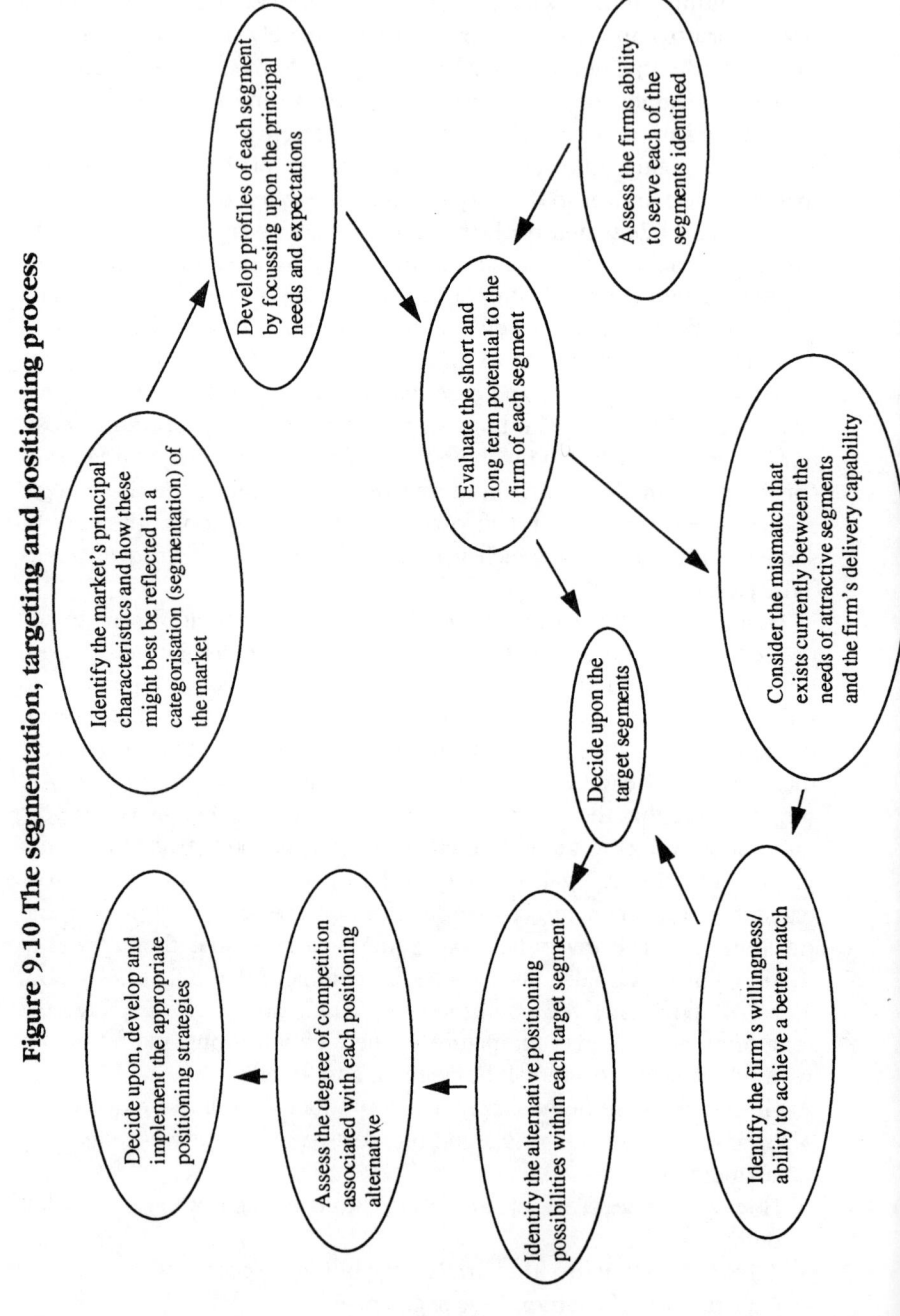

Figure 9.11 (a) Perceptions and positioning strategies of legal firms

Large and highly professional city firms ➤	Aggressively growing regional firms ➤	Medium sized regional firms growing only slowly ➤	High street solicitors
* A wide range of specialist commercial advice	* Increasing range of specialist commercial advice	* Predominantly private client work	* An emphasis upon private client work
* High fees	* Medium - high fees	* Medium fees	* Slightly old-fashioned
* Very talented staff	* High calibre staff	* Some talented individuals but also some dead wood	* Adherence to traditional values
* Good infrastructure	* Well - organised	* Woolly organisation	* Strong contacts locally based on personal relationships, weak contacts regionally and nationally
* Strong network of contacts nationally/ internationally	* Clear and focused vision and strategy with emphasis on implementation	* Desire to be big without a clear strategy for this	
	* Strong network of contacts regionally/ nationally/internationally	* Essentially a gathering of sole practitioners with some mutual interests	
		* Good contacts locally and regionally based on personal relationships	

Figure 9.11 (b)

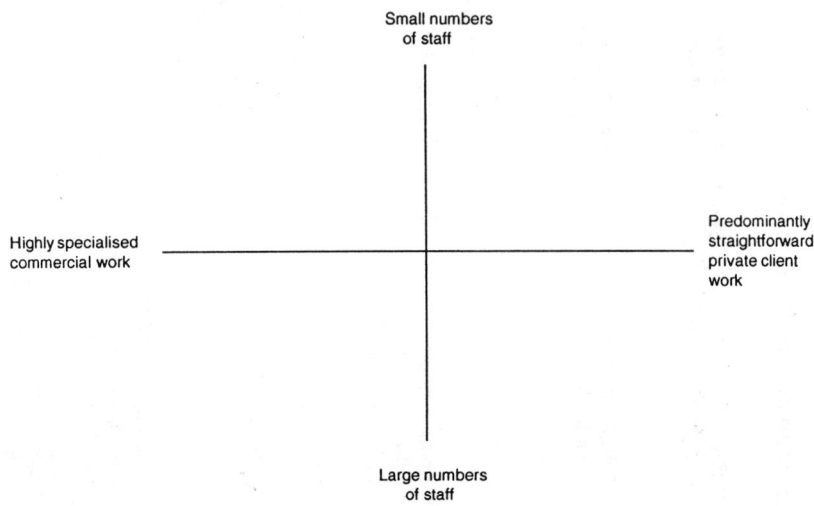

- To what extent do we *really* tailor the firm's effort to the specific needs and expectations of the segments that we deal with currently?
- What scope exists for focusing in greater detail upon the specifics of these differences and then reflecting this in our marketing effort?
- Which segments appear to offer the greatest future potential?
- What would we need to do in order to target these segments and capitalise upon this potential? Are we/would we be willing to make the sorts of investment in staff and facilities that would be needed to do this?
- What positioning stance do we adopt currently? (In thinking about this, give consideration both to the firm's general or overall stance *and* to the specific stance in each of your principal market segments). What positioning approach might be more appropriate? What would be needed in order to achieve this?

SUMMARY

Within this chapter we have focused upon the nature and importance of the various elements of the marketing mix and highlighted the need to think about the ways in which the client list might be segmented and the marketing effort focused more readily.

Because the mix represents the marketing toolkit that is used to shape the profile of the firm and determine the face that is presented to the world, the need to ensure not only that each of the individual elements has been properly developed, but also that they have then been pulled together into a coherent whole is paramount. Any failure to do this is likely to lead to wasted opportunities and a less than optimal performance. However, the reality in many firms is not only that varying degrees of attention are paid to the individual elements, but that only rarely is any real attempt made to pull these together in a truly coordinated fashion.

Recognising this, ask yourself the following questions:

1 How frequently do we review in detail each of the individual elements of the mix?
2 How clearly stated are the objectives for each element?
3 What attention has been paid to the development of an explicit marketing mix action plan?
4 To what extent is there a clear strategy for pulling together the individual elements in the form of an integrated and fully coordinated marketing programme?
5 Who has the overall responsibility for managing the mix?
6 How might the client list be segmented and the marketing effort focused more firmly? What benefits might this lead to?

CHAPTER 10

Setting the standards of client care: the Blackpool rock phenomenon

> Having read this chapter, you should:
> - understand what contributes to the total client experience;
> - appreciate the nature of the interaction between the application of legal skills and supporting skills; and
> - be aware of what would be required of your firm if you were to develop an effective customer (client) care programme.

CLIENTS ARE CUSTOMERS TOO

We commented in Chapter 9 that clients generally take their solicitor's level of legal competence for granted and that because of this the support elements of the firm are capable of taking on what some solicitors consider to be an unrealistic or unfair degree of importance in determining not just how the firm is perceived generally, but also how good (or bad) the legal skill dimensions really are. Given this, the argument for focusing upon what we can refer to as the *total client experience* is inescapable, since it is this which provides the framework for establishing the standards of overall care that clients – your customers – will perceive that they are getting from the firm.

There are several reasons why the broader aspects of client/customer care have increased in importance in recent years, although perhaps the most important and most obvious of these are the generally higher expectations of service that now exist throughout society and an apparent reduction in the willingness of members of the public to make allowances for what they see to be unreasonable or unacceptable behaviour. Couple this with the public's generally greater willingness to complain and take their custom elsewhere, and the arguments for a client care policy become ever more apparent.

Setting the standards of client care

THE BLACKPOOL ROCK PHENOMENON

It needs to be emphasised from the outset that customer care has moved on considerably from the 'have a nice day' – and indeed the 'come back soon, missing you already' – approach that characterised numerous care programmes in the early days. Instead, we are concerned here with establishing the standards that will run right the way through the firm (the Blackpool rock phenomenon), and achieving the degree of professionalism across the entire spectrum of the framework within which every aspect of firm-client interaction takes place.

Because of the way in which any truly effective client care programme for the firm straddles both the legal skills and the support

Figure 10.1 The reality - intent - capability gap

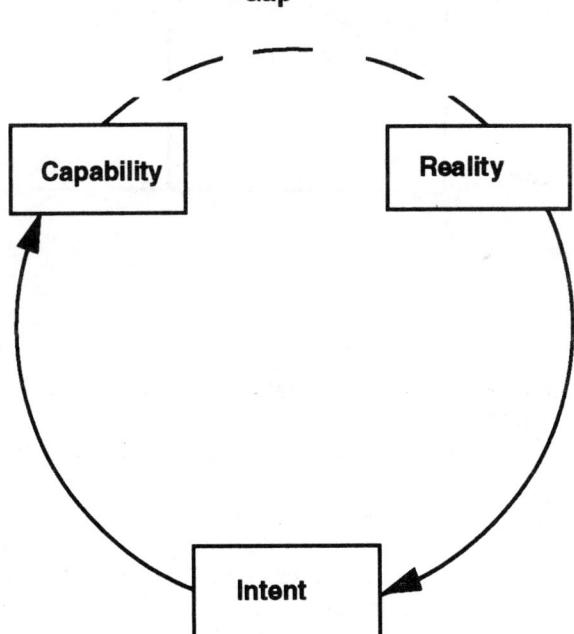

Figure 10.2 The legal/non-legal delivery matrix

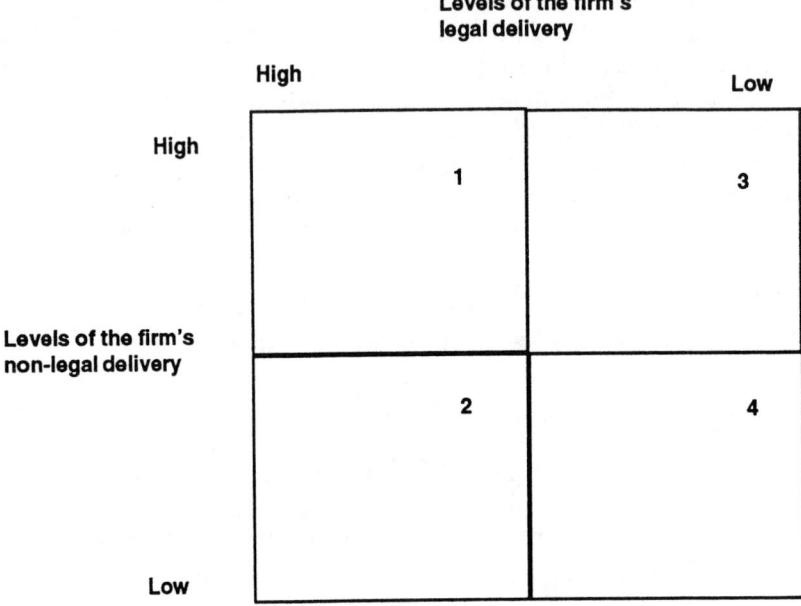

skills dimensions of the firm, you need to begin by considering three fundamental questions:

1. What sort of total experience do you give clients currently? (the reality)
2. What sort of total experience would you like to give? (the intent)
3. What are you really capable of delivering? (the capability)

This reality - intent - capability framework is illustrated in figure 10.1 and provides a basis for thinking about the size and significance of the gap that exists between intent and capability. There are, of course, numerous factors that can contribute to this gap and having identified its size, significance and the nature of the contributory factors within the firm, thought needs to be given not just to the ways in which the gap might be filled, but also to whether the firm would be willing to allocate the level of resources that would be needed to do this. In making this comment, we have several thoughts in mind, perhaps the most significant of which is that in virtually every professional firm we have visited, the partners and staff have talked about excellence and providing the very highest levels of client care. The reality, of course, is that what we can refer to as the Rolls Royce approach is only rarely feasible (or cost effective) and you need therefore to temper your ideas with a dose of reality. To help with this, turn to figure 10.2 and, being brutally honest with yourself, plot where the firm is currently, *and why*. It might be the case, for example, that you are in cell 2 (high standards of legal delivery) but because of antiquated premises, an archaic telephone system, and a dragon of a receptionist, you have relatively poor levels of support. Having identified the causes in as much detail as possible, you can then begin thinking about what would be required to move the firm either to another cell (presumably cell 1) or to a stronger and more favourable position within the existing cell.

THE LESSONS FROM ELSEWHERE

In our work with a variety of different types of organisations, there has proved to be one issue over the past few years that managers have discussed with seemingly greater passion than anything else: the standards of customer care and services that their organisations deliver. Almost without exception, every organisation we have dealt with – at least in the first instance – has claimed almost unparalleled levels of customer care, something which has led us to conclude that the business world is full of managers with a seemingly infinite capacity for self-delusion. There are, of course, exceptions to this and it is to these sorts of organisation that we now need to turn with a view to learning what it is that contributes to a truly effective customer care programme. However, before doing this, turn to figure 10.3 and think about your experiences in recent weeks as a customer of various types of organisation.

Having done this, think about the sorts of organisations which consistently achieve high levels of customer care and what it is that appears to contribute to this. In the case of the high street, for example, organisations such as Marks and Spencer, Sainsbury's and McDonald's have been at the forefront in establishing – and maintaining – the levels of service which others simply dream about. In all three cases, the factors which have led to this are straightforward and come down, firstly, to a fundamental belief on the part of senior management in the importance of customer satisfaction, and then, secondly, to the communication of these values to everyone in the organisation. High levels of service – and hence satisfaction – therefore become the norm in these circumstances rather than the exception.

> **Figure 10.3 Your experiences of customer care**
>
> Think of three organisations that you have dealt with recently.
>
> - What good and bad experiences do you remember?
>
> - Which of these were related to the behaviour of staff and which to the physical aspects of the place such as appearance, cleanliness and atmosphere?
>
> - Did there appear to be any real understanding of 'delight' factors (a 'delight' factor is something that makes you feel especially pleased)?
>
> - When you felt that you were treated either badly or less than very well, what was the effect on you?
>
> - Did you bother to complain about poorish service (poor rather than appalling) or did you simply think that you don't intend helping them to make improvements and that in the future you will go elsewhere?
>
> - When you have been treated badly or less than perfectly and the organisation has been aware of this, what efforts have been made to put things right?
>
> - If you have to go back to a place where you have had a poor experience, what attitudes do you take with you?
>
> - Do you think that most people would react to these experiences in much the same way?

By contrast, the major banks seem to operate according to a completely different set of principles altogether. Instead of being open when customers want (9 - 6 Monday to Saturday and 10 - 5 on Sunday), opening hours reflect staff demands, banking pressures and historical idiosyncrasies. Equally, at the times of highest demand (12 - 1.30), staff take lunch breaks and queues form in the branches.

Faced with critical comments such as these, bankers tend to respond by saying, "But you don't understand our problems". This sort of response is, however, a nonsense and makes a mockery of any claims of customer service. It is also one of the reasons why the building societies, which do have longer opening hours and manage to present a far friendlier face, consistently score far better than the banks in surveys of customer perceptions of care, approachability and friendliness.

The significance of the role played by senior management is these organisations in establishing the standards of service and customer care should never ever be underestimated, something which has been highlighted by the American management guru, Tom Peters. Peters' view is straightforward and unequivocal:

> "Claims of quality and customer service mean nothing unless the person at the top of the organisation is committed to them twenty four hours a day, seven days a week, fifty two weeks a year. If you compromise on this even once, you know it, your staff know it and, worst of all, your customers know it."

The implications of this for law firms and the need for absolute and total commitment on the part of the senior and/or managing partner to the quality of the total client experience are (or should be) self-evident.

CLIENT CARE IN LAW FIRMS

Relating these points to law firms was first touched upon in Chapter 3 in which we discussed the client-oriented firm and is not necessarily as difficult as it might appear at first sight. It does, however, involve running the firm for the convenience of the clients rather than, say, the solicitors (this is the equivalent of running the banks for the convenience of the customers rather than the bank staff). In the case of office hours, for example, our experiences have shown that in most instances they were established by the partners themselves several years ago and reflect what is convenient for them rather than what is necessarily the most convenient for their clients. In making this comment, we are not arguing for wholesale changes in office hours, but rather for an assessment of whether scope exists for small changes that would prove useful from the clients' point of view. Given this, consider the questions in figure 10.4.

In the light of your answers, what picture of the firm do you think emerges and what *overall* level of client care do you think the firm manages to achieve?

Figure 10.4 The initial client care audit

- Do those around you *always* behave professionally towards clients and all other members of staff? If not, what sorts of problems exist, *and why?*

- What patterns of behaviour in the firm do you consider to be unprofessional? What steps have been and are being taken in order to overcome these?

- What do you do in your firm if a client goes away obviously unhappy because of the ways in which they have been treated?

- What do you know about the reasons why some clients opt to move to another firm?

Do you and your staff............

- always acknowledge clients/visitors as soon as possible (including answering the telephone) and use their name? (In the case of the telephone, you might consider introducing a guideline that the phone will always be answered on or before the third ring between, say, 8.30 in the morning and 6 in the evening)

- welcome the clients and are invariably friendly?

- attempt to reassure them if they are anxious?

- apologise if there is a delay and give an explanation for the delay?

- explain things to them and check that they understand?

- listen to them and check that you understand what they have told you?

- have any sort of follow up process to ensure that the client is satisfied with everything he or she received from the firm?

DEVELOPING A PLAN TO IMPROVE CLIENT CARE

Having gone through the initial audit, you can then turn your attention to the ways in which a programme of client care can be developed. In doing this, you need to follow a simple four-step procedure: this is illustrated in figure 10.5.

Stage 1: The starting point

As a first step, you need to understand in detail how clients (customers) feel about the firm currently, what their expectations are and the extent to which these expectations are not being met. Although you have already completed the initial audit in figure 10.4, and indeed plotted the position of the firm in figure 10.2, consider the following additional questions:
- In the light of our comments and questions throughout the book, is the firm fundamentally client oriented or partner oriented? (in answering this, you might find it useful to refer back to figures 3.3 and 3.6).
- Do the partners *really* accept that the whole image and physical appearance of the firm is important in contributing to client care?
- Are you clear about what clients *really* want from the firm?
- What impression do clients get of the firm when they walk through the door?
- Is it likely that they find any aspect of the firm intimidating or off-putting?
- Do you have any formal mechanism currently which allows clients' views to be fed back and influence how the firm operates? (If in answering this the answer is no, refer back to Chapter 4 in which we discussed the role of marketing research as a means of measuring levels of client satisfaction)

Stage 2: Setting the standards

Having identified how clients see the firm currently, you need then to turn to the question of the overall standards of client care that you want to aim for. In this, we are assuming that the standards of professional competence are satisfactory. You should therefore focus upon the range of other factors that influence attitudes and performance such as:
- Is the reception area untidy?
- Is there a good selection of up-to-date and varied reading material?

Figure 10.5 Planning client care

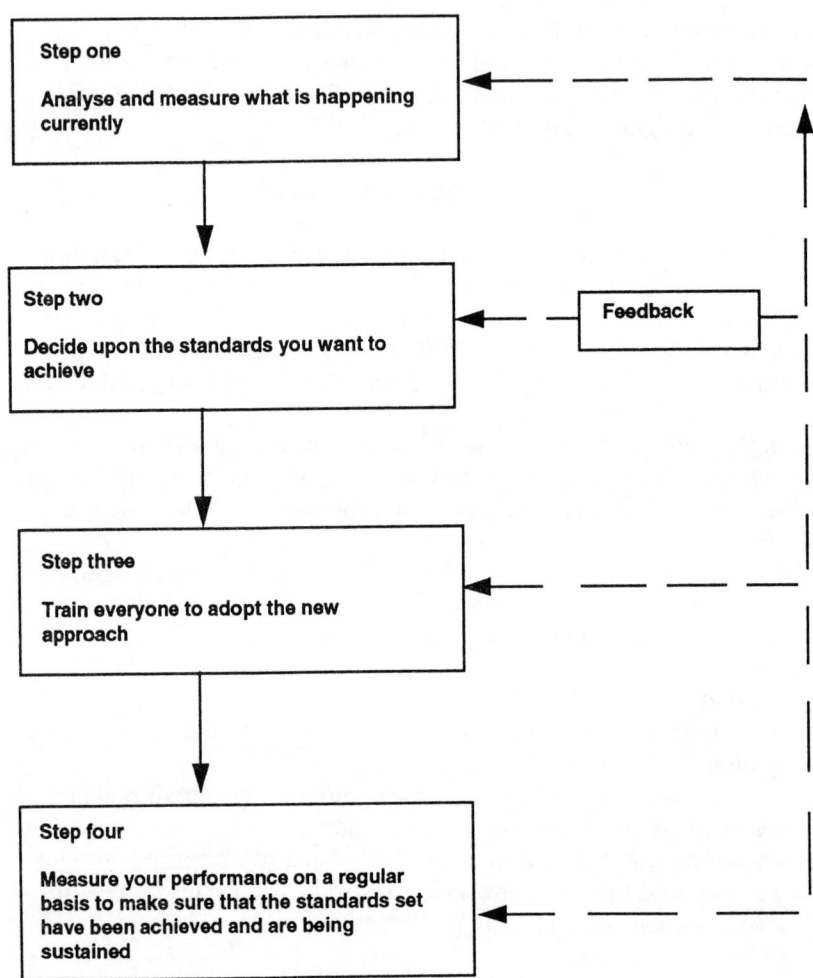

- Is the reception desk a fortress? Does the reception area have distracting or unclear notices?
- Do the reception staff appear welcoming and confident?
- Are the fee earners' rooms clean, modern and efficient?
- Do the fee earners appear welcoming and confident?
- Do all staff have a good telephone manner and is the phone answered promptly?
- Are appointments easily available and do you have a plan if they are not?
- Do you make sure that all forms of communication with clients are clear and unambiguous?
- How long do clients normally have to wait for an appointment?
- How often do appointment times overrun and by what amount?
- How accurate is the clients' record system?
- How accessible is the records system?
- How accessible are the solicitors both in and out of office hours?

In the case of your relationships with external providers, think about the answers to the following questions:
- In general terms, how do your major providers of specialist advice and services such as barristers compare with each other in terms of standards and access?
- Where you have an option, are you encouraging referrals to the very best providers or is there a tendency to make use of the same providers each time?
- How can you bring the needs of the firm and its clients more fully to the attention of the providers?
- What major strengths and weaknesses does each provider have?
- What are you doing to exploit these strengths?
- Where there are weaknesses, what are you doing to try alternatives?
- Are there opportunities to work more closely with the best providers?
- What are you doing to bring this about?
- What changes do you expect to see amongst providers over the next two years and the next five years? What are the implications of this?
- Who is specifically responsible for assessing your internal data to provide a clear picture of provider success?
- What gaps in information do you have?
- What are you doing to set up a system to provide the information?

Against this background, you can then move on to stage three and to the ways in which a client care programme can be implemented.

Stage 3: Planning and implementing the customer care programme

In planing how to implement a new and higher level of client care, you need to focus upon five areas:

1 *Developing a client oriented mission statement* Make sure that the firm's mission statement includes an explicit expression of the level of client care you are aiming for. An example of this might be:

> "As a family firm, our staff are committed to providing the very highest level of legal care for our clients and ensuring that this is consistent with their short and long term needs."

2 *Involving the staff at all stages* Having made a statement of the standards you are aiming for, make sure that staff throughout the firm understand this, believe in it and know how it will be achieved. Make sure also that they feel a sense of ownership. In order to achieve this, make sure that as many staff as possible are involved in deciding what should and needs to be done. There are several ways of doing this, including getting all the staff to complete a questionnaire concerned with what they believe or know of what clients might want from the firm. Other methods of getting ideas involve brainstorming and wide ranging discussion groups to identify the sorts of changes needed.

3 *Defining the requirements of the key activities* For certain key activities such as answering the telephone, giving instructions and making appointments define *exactly* what is required and develop procedures to ensure that the activity is carried out in the same way by everyone every time.

4 *Confirm that all staff are part of the client management process* Clients should know who all staff are. One way of doing this is by the reception staff having a degree of uniformity in what they wear (perhaps even a uniform) and everyone wearing name badges. Think also about putting up a board in the waiting room with photographs and names so that clients can identify who is who and what they do. Remember that Practice Rule 15 requires that clients be told whom they are dealing with. There can therefore be an opportunity to introduce the 'team' who will ordinarily work on the file(s), something which quite apart from the benefit of giving clients several

named individuals to contact when necessary, can act as a team-building and a motivating exercise for the staff if approached in the right spirit.

The plan needs also to ensure that the role that staff play within the team is continually developed and reinforced, with clear guidelines being given regarding the limits of their authority. However, it is worth remembering that many fee earners only use their secretaries as typists, which overburdens the fee earner and under-uses that the talents that their secretaries generally possess. Try therefore to devise standard letters and procedures that need minimal dictation and supervision. You will probably be agreeably surprised at the extra output and job satisfaction that you can both achieve without either of you working any harder.

5 *Staff Training* It is essential that all staff – legal and support – are trained to the right level and that training is continually maintained by the use of refresher courses. In the case of new staff it is essential that they understand from the outset what is expected of them. All too often, however, the approach adopted in many firms is that the newest member of the support staff is thrown in at the deep end in what is very often one of the most critical positions – answering the telephone. Whilst there are always pressures to make sure that staff are productive as quickly as possible, any new starter needs to be trained in the basic procedures before being let loose.

In many cases, the staff who prove most resistant to client care training are those who have been in the firm the longest, believing that they should not be treated as learners along with the new recruits. However, if you are to achieve a high standard of client care across the firm as a whole, all staff need to be made fully aware of what you are aiming for and what their good and bad behaviour patterns are. Recognising this, never compromise by giving in to individual members of staff and allowing them to miss out on the training sessions. Instead, use them as the basis for team building as well as developing newly focused client care skills.

Having gone through the training process, think then about the ways in which effective performance can be highlighted and rewarded. One of the easiest and most effective ways of doing this is to ensure that any favourable comments from clients are passed on or shared with the relevant staff members. If you are conducting client satisfaction surveys, you will still probably have favourable remarks passed by clients in letters or verbally, and you have the chance to 'share the glory' with others. Research consistently confirms the importance of recognition of achievement as an important motivator leading to increased job satisfaction, and indirectly to ever higher levels of client care.

Stage 4: Measuring the firm's performance

Having set out to develop a client care programme, you need to monitor progress and performance on a regular basis. At the outset, therefore, identify your ten most important client care dimensions and then, using the sorts of techniques that we discussed in Chapter 4, measure your performance on these on either a monthly or a quarterly basis. Having got this information, you need then to make use of it by feeding back the good and the bad points to everyone in the firm and, where appropriate, identify the sorts of changes that need to be made to get back on target.

In the case of high street retailing, one of the most consistently effective ways of measuring customer care performance has proved to be by means of 'mystery shoppers.' The mystery shopper (MS), who is either an employee from head office or a market researcher, is used by the retailer to explore particular parts of the operation such as the returns policy, the ways in which difficult customers are handled, and the ability of staff to cope with problems at periods of peak demand. The MS therefore goes into the shop, behaves like a customer, and then feeds the details of the experiences, be they good or bad, back to head office.

Although we are not making out a case here for mystery clients, there are several lessons that can be learned from this, but particularly the need to take an objectively detailed and, in the real sense of the word, naive look at various parts of the firm *from the clients' point of view*. It is in this way that you can build up a far clearer picture and understanding of what is going right and what is going wrong. (If this idea appeals to you then you can obtain a self-test pack from the Law Society (Eastern Region) at DX 5880 Cambridge (telephone 0223 328924) for a few pounds.)

SUMMARY

Within this chapter, we have highlighted the sorts of issues that need to be taken into account in developing a client care programme within the firm. As with many of the initiatives that we have discussed in earlier chapters, you need to identify clearly what your objectives are and

Setting the standards of client care

then, having determined how these will be achieved, ensure that there is total commitment from across the firm and that the responsibility for driving the programme forward is clearly allocated. Given this, think about the following questions which are then pulled together in the form of a customer care action plan in figure 10.6.

- Do you handle your clients in a way that you can be proud of?
- As a firm, do you have a clear and agreed view of the sort of client care policy that would really be appropriate?
- What is needed in order to implement this?
- Who will take on the responsibility for driving it?
- Do you ensure that your providers are fully aware of the dimensions and standards of your client care programme?
- Do you put sufficient pressure upon providers such as barristers to ensure that they also have an effective client care policy and that it matches your expectations?

Figure 10.6 The client care action plan

Our client care policy is:

The weaknesses in our current approach are:
-
-
-
-
-

To overcome these weaknesses, we need to take action in the following areas:

Action areas	**Timescales**	**Responsibility**
•		
•		
•		
•		
•		
•		

(continued)

The performance measures that will be used to monitor our progress are:

Performance measures   **Responsibility**

Monthly

-
-
-

Quarterly

-
-
-

Annually

-
-
-

CHAPTER 11

Internal marketing, leadership and teamworking: fighting the Napoleonic complex

Having read this chapter, you should:
- understand what is meant by internal marketing;
- appreciate the significance of the contribution that internal marketing can make to the effective working of the firm;
- recognise the importance of vision, strategy and leadership;
- have a greater understanding of what contributes to more effective teams; and
- appreciate some of the issues associated with effective leadership.

A point that we have made at several stages in this book is that all too often plans either falter or fail because of the difficulties associated with their implementation. Recognition of this has led in recent years to a considerable amount of attention having been paid to the ways in which internal marketing, team building and particular styles of leadership can make the process of implementing a plan both easier and more effective. It is to these three areas that we now turn our attention.

VISION, STRATEGY AND LEADERSHIP

Having worked with a wide variety of organisations over the years, we believe strongly that it is possible to distinguish between good and bad organisations – that is those that are effective and those that are ineffective – by examining them against the background of the deceptively simple model that is illustrated in figure 11.1.

The thinking behind the model is straightforward. If an organisation, regardless of its type or size, is to move ahead effectively, it is essential that those running it have a clear *vision* of the sort of organisation

Figure 11.1 Vision, strategy and leadership

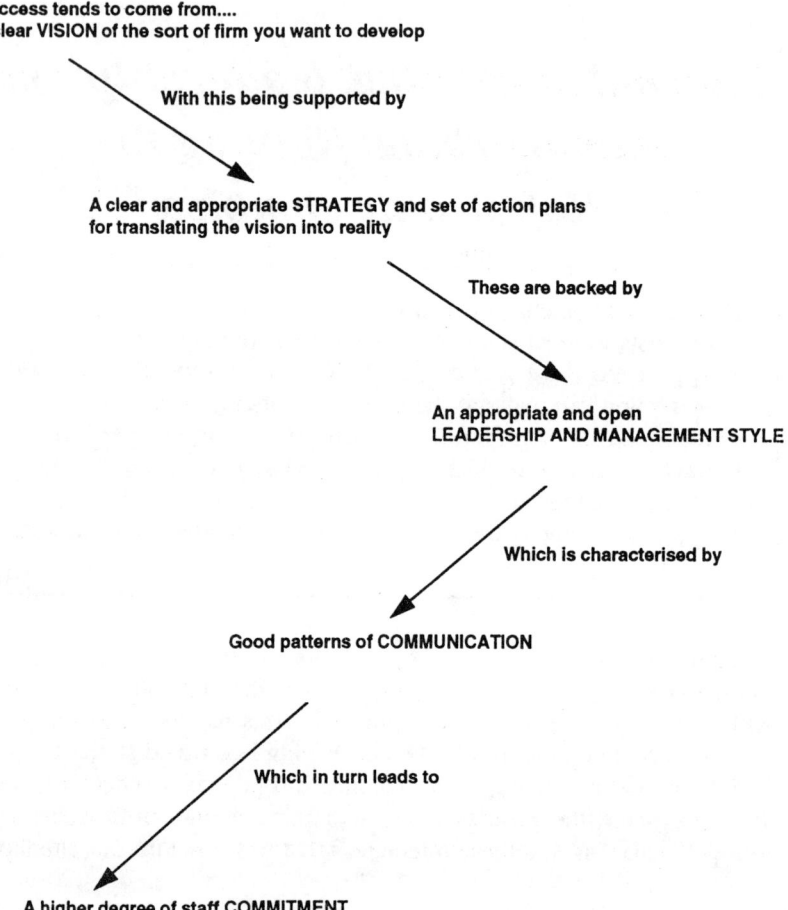

they are trying to develop; that there is a clear *strategy* and set of action plans for achieving this; and that a clear and appropriate *leadership/management* style exists. These are then reinforced by open patterns of *communication* so that the staff are fully aware of the direction in which the organisation is going, what is expected of them and how they will benefit. Given this, *levels of commitment* are likely to increase substantially.

In the light of this model, there are several questions that you need to consider; these appear in figure 11.2.

Quite deliberately, we have not asked any questions in figure 11.2 about levels of commitment, since it should be apparent by now that the commitment of staff will be influenced to a very substantial degree by the leadership/management styles and patterns of communication that exist. However, before going any further and discussing how levels of commitment might be increased by internal marketing, it is worth taking a step sideways and looking at the work in the 1950s of Douglas McGregor and in particular his development of Theory X and Theory Y. In essence, McGregor argues that there are few inherently bad employees, but plenty of bad managers. People, he suggested, typically have the capacity for self motivation and that in general it is the management styles and organisational structures and constraints which inhibit this and prevent them from making a worthwhile contribution; these ideas are summarised in figure 11.3.

It follows from this, and indeed from the earlier part of the chapter, that the firm is likely to work in a far more effective manner if certain broad guidelines are adhered to. An important starting point in this is the development of open patterns of communication with staff being kept fully aware of how the organisation is developing. Two immediately valuable tools for this are internal marketing and the development of teams. However, before looking at these two areas, ask yourself the question: which of McGregor's two theories most closely typifies ways of thinking within your firm?

SO WHAT IS INTERNAL MARKETING ?

The idea of internal marketing is straightforward and based on the idea that an organisation will operate far more effectively if its staff have a clear understanding of core values and objectives and are able to identify with these. To achieve this empathy, there is a need to recruit appropriate people, give them a strong sense of identity and operating freedom, and support them with good patterns of communication and open management styles. Assuming this is done properly, the pay-offs

Figure 11.2 The vision, strategy, leadership and communication checklist

The vision
- How clear a vision exists of the sort of firm that you and your partners are trying to develop? (In answering this, you might refer back to our discussion of the importance of vision in Chapter 7.)
- To what extent is this vision clouded either by disharmony between the partners or a failure to discuss it in detail?
- Given your location, resources and any other constraints, how realistic is this vision?
- How effectively has this vision been communicated to staff throughout the firm?

The strategy and action plan
- How well thought out are the action plans?
- How explicit are they?
- How well resourced are they?
- How well have patterns of responsibility been allocated?

The leadership/management styles
- What sort of leadership/management styles exist within the firm?
- What degree of balance (or imbalance) is there between the different styles of the partners?
- How appropriate are these styles, given the sorts of staff that you have and the anticipated demands of the mid to late 1990s?
- How do the staff perceive these styles?
- What evidence is there of dissatisfaction with them?

Communication
- How well developed are the patterns of communication within the firm?
- Does information flow in all directions?
- What obstacles to good information flow exist?
- What communication-related problems have been encountered?

> ### Figure 11.3 McGregor's Theory X and Theory Y
>
> Working in the 1950s, McGregor identified two patterns of thought and assumptions about people in organisations.
>
> Theory X argues that people are:
> - inherently lazy and work as little as possible
> - lacking in ambition, dislike responsibility and prefer to be led
> - self-centred, indifferent to organisational needs, and resistant to change
> - gullible and not very bright
>
> By contrast, theory Y suggests that people:
> - are not by nature passive or resistant to organisational needs, but have become so as the result of their experiences in organisations
> - have an enormous capacity for motivation, development and responsibility, and that structures and systems need to be designed to reflect this and reduce the constraints and levels of control

can be considerable and are likely to be reflected in far higher levels of motivation and commitment (these ideas were first touched upon in our discussion in Chapter 1 of the 7-S framework).

In the light of these comments, consider the questions that appear below:
- Do the staff really understand the firm's core values and objectives and empathise with them?
- Do you feel that you really have the right type and blend of staff within the firm?
- Do you spend enough time training staff and equipping them with the skills needed?
- How often are problems caused by poor communications?
- Do your staff feel that they have sufficient operating freedom?
- Are the patterns of communication sufficiently open?
- How involved are your staff in deciding how the firm is run?

Against the background of your answers to these questions, think about the sorts of leadership styles that exist within the firm (these are discussed again at a later stage in this chapter in figures 11.5 and 11.6).

Are they, for example, essentially a reflection of a 'tells' approach in which having made a decision, you and your colleagues simply tell the staff what to do, or is it rather more of a 'sells' style in which you sell the idea to others by discussing it in some detail and giving consideration to the implications for them? Another possible approach is the consultative style in which you only make the decision after having discussed the various aspects with those who are involved or who are likely to be affected. Internal marketing gives full recognition to the need to carry staff with you and therefore the crucial importance of making sure that patterns of communication are as open as possible and that staff feel a strong sense of involvement; without this, it is likely that you are simply failing to exploit the real potential of the firm and the people in it. You might therefore care to reflect upon the fact that it is widely acknowledged that investment in people and training are the two essential components of total quality management. This is reflected, for example, in the preamble to BS 7850 which deals with TQM.

THE ROLE OF TEAMS WITHIN THE FIRM

As part of the overall process of internal marketing and improving the effectiveness of the firm, you need to give explicit consideration to the scope that exists for teamworking and to the nature of any blocks to teamworking that exist currently. In doing this, you need to recognise that every member of staff is or should be capable of making a direct or indirect contribution to the effective treatment of a client. In making this comment, we are returning to the idea that it is not simply the legal aspects of the consultation that lead to clients going away satisfied or dissatisfied, but that the non-legal elements that surround the consultation, and in particular, the support staff, are often capable of exerting a powerful influence upon clients' perceptions. Recognition of this highlights the crucial importance of teams and teamworking throughout the firm.

The pros and cons of teamworking

The benefits that can come from teamworking can be substantial and include:
- The support that colleagues can give to individuals so that they can more easily work to their strengths;
- The ways in which teams can build upon the different ideas and skills which individual members of the team possess;

- The ways in which the team can capitalise upon the previous experiences of staff in doing a similar job in different circumstances;
- The discovery of particular skills which in normal circumstances might be hidden, but which frequently emerge when teamworking;
- The ways in which, by ensuring staff familiarise themselves with colleagues' jobs, the firm can avoid an overdependence on individuals, reduce the load on some staff members at times of crisis, and reduce the risk of procedures being carried out differently and incorrectly;
- Ensuring that clients can gain from a better 'experience' in a visit to the firm through a more highly coordinated approach;
- A sense of shared purpose and the general levels of synergy that teams can achieve.

There are also, of course, some potential dangers of teamworking which can cause problems:
- It can expose the weaknesses of some members of staff and reinforce the egos and positions of those members of staff who see themselves as 'experts;'
- To be successful, teamworking requires staff to alternate between leading, supporting and perhaps being on the sidelines at different times and this continual change in relationships can prove difficult for some staff to handle.

However, on balance, the pros of teamworking outweigh any possible cons by a substantial margin. Recognising this, the question that needs to be considered is how more effective teams can be developed within the firm.

Building more effective teams

Only rarely, if ever, is there an opportunity to build a team from scratch and, in many firms, there are relatively infrequent opportunities even to modify teams other than at the margin when, for example, someone leaves and you bring in someone new. It is possible, however, to make adjustments by controlling some members of staff, encouraging others in a certain direction and, when recruiting, doing it with a deep-seated understanding of the balances and imbalances that exist within different parts of the firm currently. The sorts of questions that can help in this by providing a greater insight to your existing teams appear in figure 11.4. Remember, therefore, that when forming or building a team, you need to aim for a blend of strengths, skills and personalities and should avoid building one that simply reinforces the status quo.

> **Figure 11.4 The teamworking checklist**
>
> - What teams do you have within the firm currently?
> - Do you make as much use of teams as you might?
> - How well do your teams work currently?
> - What obstacles to better teamworking exist?
> - Do you have well balanced teams or do they appear to be dominated by particular individuals?
> - What changes would be needed in order to achieve a better balance of skills?
> - Do the members of the teams appear to have sufficiently complementary skills?
> - What appear to be the attitudes and levels of motivation of various team members currently? Do they need to be modified in any way? (Do not assume that good working relationships automatically lead to effectiveness. Indeed they can lead to a degree of complacency in which old working practices and conventional wisdoms are never challenged or changed for the better).
> - How are junior staff treated and what roles do they appear to be playing within the teams? Are they simply being tolerated or are real efforts being made by other team members to use their skills and develop their abilities?

So what contributes to more effective teams?

The guidelines for building more effective teams are relatively straightforward and include:
- ensuring that the team has a distinct and measurable purpose
- providing constructive feedback on performance
- varying the team's tasks and responsibilities over time
- rotating staff on a periodic and planned basis so that new talents and ideas are injected to the team and that the membership and patterns of thinking do not become too incestuous or complacent
- gradually increasing the degree of autonomy
- encouraging the team to redefine their responsibilities and tasks.

Against the background of these comments, consider the following questions:
- Do you trust the members of your team?
- Do they trust you?

Internal marketing, leadership and teamworking

- Is there mutual trust?
- Do you respect the members of your team?
- Do they respect you?
- Is there mutual respect?
- Is the atmosphere open and supportive?
- Can you handle success *and* failure?
- Are work loads properly balanced?
- Are the team members loyal to you and/or to the firm and to each other?
- Is the team mutually supportive?
- Can you and other team members express true opinions?
- Do you plan, organise, review and communicate effectively?
- Does everyone feel part of the team?
- Does each team have a clear sense of direction?

ASPECTS OF LEADERSHIP: SUPERLAWYERS AND INCOMPETENT MEDDLERS

In 1994, we carried out a study amongst office managers in a number of professional firms, including solicitors, doctors and accountants. In doing this we were attempting to find out how professionals are viewed by their key staff. The findings led us to suggest that "the average professional is a poor manager who has appalling communication skills, little real idea of how to plan, fewer ideas of how to motivate staff, and typically adopts an inconsistent and idiosyncratic style of management and leadership."

These conclusions need to be seen against the general background of the work in which we examined the principal roles that professionals are typically expected to perform:
- a *professional carer (or adviser)* role
- a *leadership* role
- a *team building* and *team player* role

Although the majority of those surveyed seemed to feel that their solicitors carried out the professional adviser role fairly well, they proved to be far less complimentary about the extent to which the leadership and team roles were either recognised or performed. It was this that then led us to categorise solicitors along the two dimensions that we first introduced in Chapter 6 (their *willingness* to manage and their *ability* to manage) and to label them as superlawyers, dangerlawyers, opt-outs or incompetent meddlers (this was illustrated in figure 6.2).

Balancing the three roles: the problems of leadership

Although our research showed that solicitors' legal and professional adviser skills were generally (but not invariably) acknowledged by their staff, an all too common feeling amongst their managers appeared to be that they use this as an excuse both for their appalling leadership and team working skills, and for the ways in which staff are all too frequently expected to operate with a degree of telepathy.

With regard to the *leadership* role, our work suggested that interpretations of how best to do this appear to vary enormously. For some, leadership appears to mean giving orders and simply telling the staff what to do, with little or no real attempt being made to explain why or how; it was this which led us to suggest that in a surprisingly high number of instances there appeared to be a need to *fight the Napoleonic complex*. For others, but seemingly a minority, leadership proved to be a far more meaningful activity which involved developing strong and effective communication networks, giving emphasis to staff development, and ensuring that everyone understood what was expected of them. For yet others, it was something in which they showed a vague, if amateurish, interest every now and again (generally when they didn't appear to have much else to do).

A further area which led to problems of leadership was what we labelled *the closed file syndrome,* with the senior support staff being denied access to areas of information – particularly financial information – and excluded from any involvement in important decisions. Instead they were simply told the outcome of a planning meeting and then expected to show great enthusiasm and commitment to the process of implementation. Given these sorts of comments, turn to figure 11.5 and think about the sort of overall style that you exhibit.

Building and motivating the firm's teams

The third area we looked at in the research was the *team working* role and, in particular, how it is interpreted. All too often there was a failure to recognise the extent of the contribution that was needed, or indeed the considerable amount of time and effort that is involved in building, developing and maintaining effective teams. Instead, it appeared to be frequently believed either that teams would emerge as if by magic or that the sole responsibility for team building rested with others.

These problems were then exacerbated by the ways in which the *opt-outs, dangerlawyers* and *incompetent meddlers* automatically blamed staff for lost files and rarely – if ever – admitted to their mistakes.

> **Figure 11.5 Leadership styles**
>
> - The PROPHET has a vision
> - The BARBARIAN is pragmatic, forceful, action oriented
> - The BUILDER develops structures
> - The EXPLORER develops skills
> - The SYNERGIST balances skills and structures
> - The ADMINISTRATOR integrates systems to achieve the perfectly managed firm
> - The BUREAUCRAT applies tight controls, cuts costs and has no desire to be creative
> - The ARISTOCRAT inherits, does no work but upsets the team
>
> What does your response tell you about yourself?

When it came to *motivation,* solicitors appeared to perform equally badly by working on the basis that staff should not worry because they will be told when they get it wrong (good staff, it is commonly believed by many solicitors never need their egos massaging by being told when they get things right!)

The nine deadly sins

Typical of the other mistakes made which were highlighted by the study were:
- the failure to recognise that staff have work schedules and deadlines and cannot necessarily always take on extra jobs or work late
- making decisions for their own benefit without thinking of the consequences for others
- not agreeing the boundaries of staff responsibility and authority
- working on a need-to-know basis
- persisting with poor communication networks so that mistakes are repeated
- taking a 'don't bother me, I'm too busy' attitude
- breaking the rules and undermining the guidelines laid down by the practice manager
- not knowing enough about individual members of staff, their aspirations, motivations and limitations
- requiring some staff to go through the practice or office manager rather than being able to talk directly to the partners.

Now, although we know that none of these criticisms can be levelled at *you* (as the reader), you might find it useful to take each of the points in turn and think about the extent to which others within your firm are guilty of these sorts of mistakes. Having done this, think about the consequences for the staff and in particular the levels of motivation, morale and team effectiveness.

SUMMARY: SO WHAT ARE THE IMPLICATIONS OF THIS?

We started off this chapter by suggesting that the successful implementation of plans is often hampered by certain styles of leadership and poorly developed and badly managed teams, two elements which highlight the need for a programme of internal as well as external marketing. Recognising this, you need to think about how, if at all, internal marketing is manifested within the firm currently and how an internal marketing programme might possibly either be developed or improved. As part of this, give thought also to the nature of the team working and leadership styles that exist and to the scope that exists for their development and improvement. In the case of leadership styles, figure 11.6 provides a framework for categorising the predominant styles not just of the firm's solicitors, but also of others such as the office manager, the reception staff, the administrative staff, and so on. Given that a participative style is arguably the most appropriate for a professional organisation such as a law firm, you might like to consider whether you appear to have the right mix and, if not, the sorts of problems this creates and what would be involved in changing the balance.

The final issue that you need to consider at this stage is concerned with the extent to which you pay attention to internal marketing and how this might be improved. To help with this, you might go back to the seven questions that we posed earlier in the chapter in our explanation of what internal marketing involves (see page 149), and then consider how you perform in terms of what we refer to as 'the door exercise.' This is a straightforward concept and based on the idea that, like a door, management styles can be open, closed or ajar. In the case of the open door style, staff make regular and significant contributions to the development of the firm, because they know:

- how the firm works;
- what is expected of them in terms of daily routines;
- that they are encouraged to put forward their ideas;
- how their ideas and suggestions will be evaluated and used;
- what the future aims and objectives of the firm are and how they can contribute; and

Figure 11.6 The four leadership styles

	The extent of management authority	
	High	**Low**
High	**Consultative** Managers discuss the decision with others who might be involved. Having listened to these views, the manager then makes the decision.	**Participative** The manager discusses the decision with others who are involved and they take the decision jointly.
Low	**Autocratic** The manager simply makes all decisions and tells the staff what they have to do.	**Paternalistic** The manager makes the decision and then 'sells' this to those who are affected so that they understand it and will implement it with a degree of enthusiasm.

(Staff freedom and involvement in decision making: vertical axis, High to Low)

Note: The use within this matrix of the word 'manager' rather than solicitor or partner is deliberate and designed to highlight the need to manage the firm in a conscious manner rather than falling into the trap of being an opt out, incompetent meddler or dangerlawyer.

- that they would be involved if painful decisions had to be made, so that the outcome would not come as a bolt out of the blue.

In firms where the door is partially open, staff are kept informed on an irregular basis which is influenced as much by crises and mistakes as anything else. Other stimuli are one of the partners reading a book which advocates open communication and one of the partners needing the staff to rally round when problems arise.

In many ways, this is the worst situation for the staff as they never really know where they stand. One day they feel motivated and enthusiastic because their contributions have been asked for and recognised, whilst the next day they will feel ignored and insignificant. In this situation, staff are often expected to offer instant solutions to problems when crises occur, but are not expected to contribute to planning for longer term improvements, never really know if their unsolicited contributions will be welcome or scorned and don't really know what is expected of them.

Where the door is fully closed, the partners make every decision themselves and let staff have the minimum information that they need simply to perform their tasks.

The staff in this situation are very clear about their role and what is expected of them. For some, who have no real commitment to the firm, their job is simply a way of earning a salary until they find something better. For others who look for more from a job, the experience is extraordinarily frustrating. Frequently, these staff feel resentful when their intelligence is insulted and their self-respect is damaged. The partners make it obvious that they have the responsibility for every detail of the firm and as the complexity of running law firms increases, more and more problems emerge. In these circumstances staff become increasingly resentful and retreat so that they will not look for things that are going wrong and may even feel some satisfaction when a crisis occurs and a partner makes a mistake.

CHAPTER 12

Implementing the plan and making things happen

> Having read this chapter, you should:
> - understand more clearly the nature and cause of the sorts of factors that help or hinder the development and implementation of marketing plans;
> - have a greater insight to the ways in which obstacles might possibly be overcome; and
> - have developed a framework for implementing a marketing programme for your firm.

Throughout this book we have concentrated upon developing a relatively pragmatic approach which reflects an emphasis upon the sorts of issues that are associated with the development and implementation of a stronger client-centred approach to the marketing of law firms. Within this chapter we pull some of these ideas together in the form of an action plan which should provide the framework for your firm's future marketing effort.

THE BARRIERS TO IMPLEMENTATION

We have already made the observation that planning is generally a relatively straightforward activity, but that plans too often founder during their implementation phase. Although there are numerous reasons for this, the most common have proved to be over-ambitious objectives, unrealistic timescales, inadequate funding, a lack of staff (and partner) commitment and feeling of ownership to its implementation, and, perhaps most importantly, the absence of someone with sufficient authority who is willing to take on the responsibility for driving the plan on a day-to-day basis. Given these points, consider the following questions:

1 Are you at all guilty of setting objectives that whilst they look impressive, are likely to prove too ambitious? (the hopeless optimism phenomenon)
2 Are you trying to do too much in too short a time?
3 Have you really thought through the funding implications of the plan and are you confident that funding will not be a problem?
4 Are you likely to experience any skills shortages during the period covered by the plan?
5 Have you made sure that staff throughout the firm have been involved in the planning process, kept informed of what you are setting out to achieve, and are fully committed to the plan?
6 Are *all* the partners fully committed to the plan?
7 Have you allocated responsibilities properly?
8 Do you have the right person to drive the plan forward (the plan's 'champion')?
9 Have you built in the appropriate checks?
10 Have you scheduled a series of planning review meetings to monitor progress?
11 Have you given sufficient thought to the sorts of factors that might make the implementation of the plan easier and/or more effective?

Assuming that you are satisfied with the answers to these questions, you can then turn your attention to the action planning framework that is illustrated in figure 12.1; all that remains for us is to wish you happy (and successful) marketing planning!

However, in a majority of firms the planning and implementation process often proves to be a rather more difficult exercise. Given this, turn to figure 12.2 which is designed to highlight the sorts of implementation problems that you might possibly encounter. Having worked your way through the diagram, it should be apparent that there are several major potential problem areas. These include:

- failing to take sufficient account of the environment;
- overestimating what the firm is *really* capable of delivering;
- failing to recognise the real significance of staff commitment and of the need for a sense of staff ownership of the plan;
- assuming that implementation will take place even though the specific responsibility for making the various parts of the plan work has not been clearly allocated; and
- failing to recognise that even the very best plans may encounter problems or need modifying as the result of an unpredictable shift in the environment.

Recognition of these sorts of issues leads fairly logically to the ideas and process encapsulated in figure 12.3 (a) and (b).

Implementing the plan and making things happen

Figure 12.1 The marketing action planning framework

Marketing objectives (In order of priority)	Actions required	Timing	Costs	Responsibility	Interim performance measures
•					
•					
•					
•					
•					
•					

Marketing for Law Firms

Figure 12.2 Identifying possible implementation problems

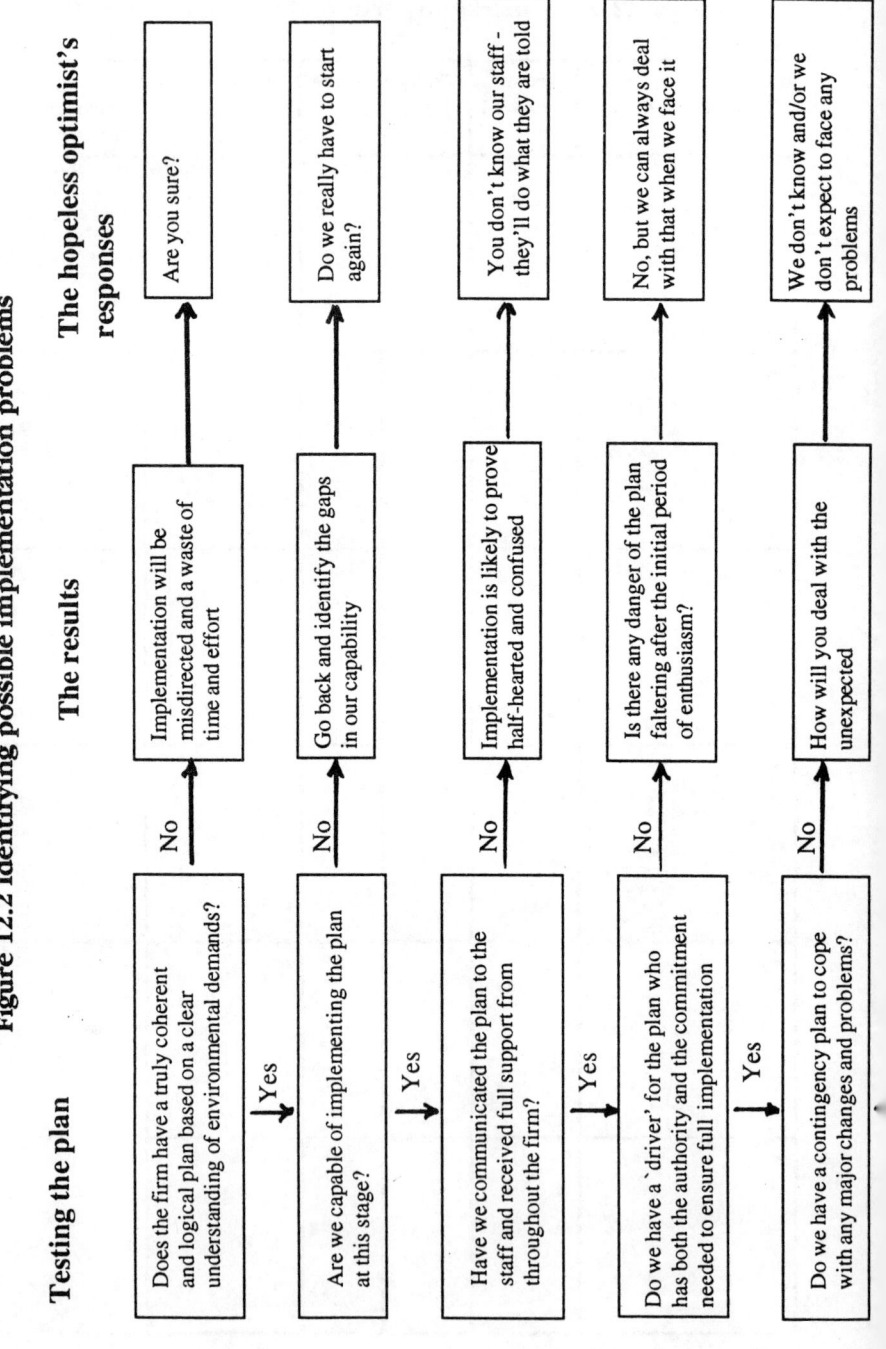

Figure 12.3 (a) Dealing with implementation problems

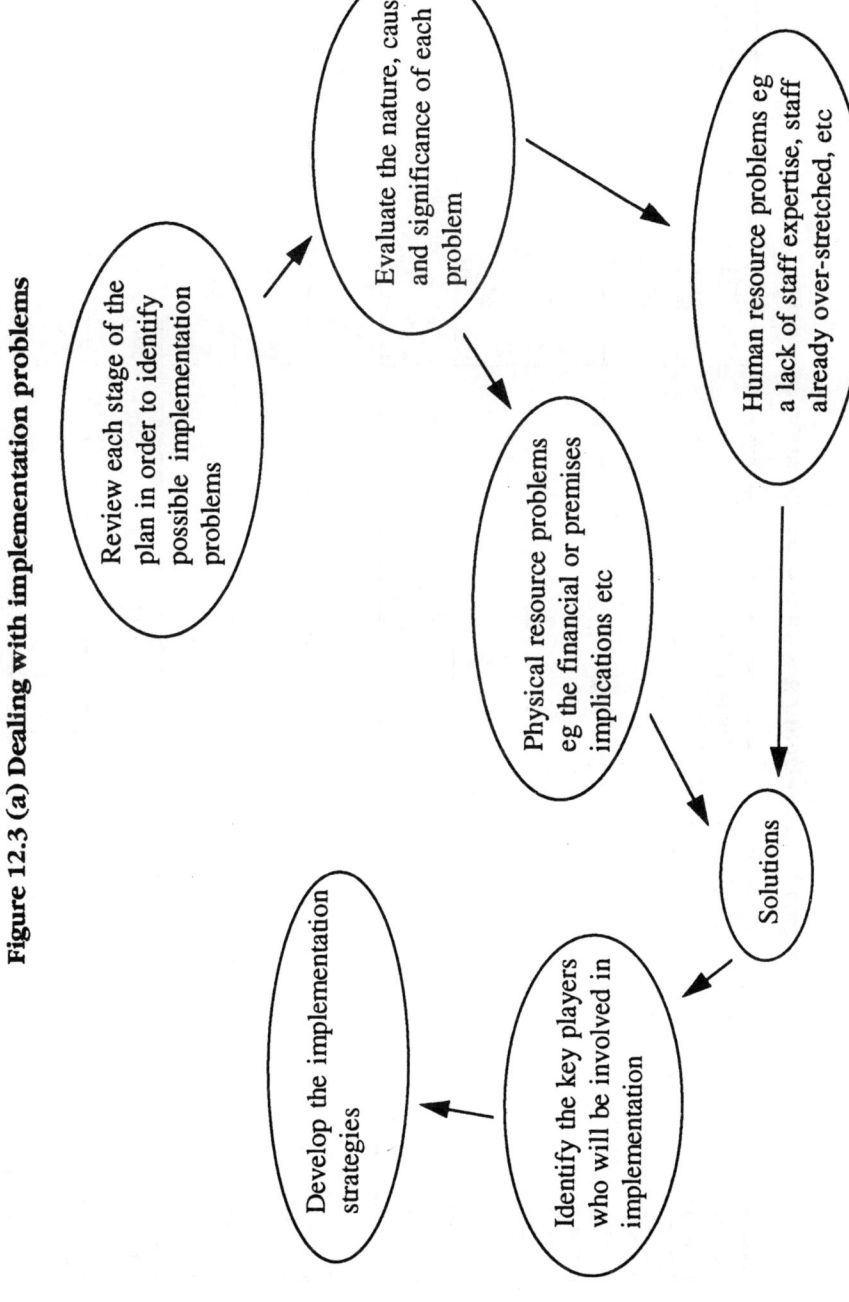

Figure 12.3 (b) Dealing with implementation problems

Factors that are likely to inhibit effective implemetation of the plan	Their significance	The actions needed to deal with the problem
*		
*		
*		
*		
*		
*		
*		
*		
*		

SUMMARY

Come to the Edge
We might fall
Come to the Edge
It's too high!
COME TO THE EDGE
And they came
and he pushed
and they flew   *(source unknown)*

CHAPTER 13

Scrivener and Proctor (Solicitors)

Scrivener and Proctor (Solicitors) is situated in an East Midlands market town of some 85,000 people. The town's population is expected to grow by around 15% over the next few years. The firm was established in 1935 and has four partners. Quite deliberately, the partners have developed or been recruited for their complementary skills, something which they believe represents a fundamental strength of the firm. The somewhat autocratic senior partner, Michael Harrison, is the firm's generalist, whilst the others have special interests in conveyancing, family law, probate and certain aspects of commercial law. The ages of the partners, all of whom are male, are 62, 64, 53 and 27.

The solicitors are supported by ageing legal executives and an articled clerk. The administration is in the hands of a 64 year old senior receptionist who has one full-time and two part-time receptionists to help her and who she rules with a rod of iron. Office hours are as follows:

    Monday - Friday   9.15 - 12.45
                                2.00 - 5.00
                         (Closed Wednesday afternoons)

The firm is based in a converted, turn of the century building which is increasingly proving to be cramped and old-fashioned. Behind the building are parking spaces for six cars, all of which are reserved for the staff. The nearest public car park is 300 metres away but, because of its proximity to the town centre, this is often full. A bus route passes the office door and there is a bus stop fifty metres away.

The building's ground floor consists of a reception and waiting area and one of the four partners' offices. The other offices and the toilets are on the first and second floors. The reception staff work from behind a chest-high counter. Having reported to reception, clients sit in the waiting area until their solicitor is free; this is announced by a flashing light, a buzzer and the receptionist calling out the name of the client who is then pointed in the direction of the solicitor's office.

Clients' records are non-existent except for deeds and wills. When a client file is opened the only two people in the office who know about it are the relevant fee earner and his secretary. The telephone system was last updated five years ago and, with too few lines, is increasingly being found to be inadequate, with the result that it is often difficult to make an external call. Equally, clients frequently find the lines to be engaged when trying to make an appointment.

A rival firm has recently opened an office 300 yards away in a new purpose-built building complete with car park. Its three partners have developed a strong reputation for their legal skills and friendly and up-to-date approach. Because of this, Scrivener and Proctor (Solicitors) has recently lost a number of its clients, including several of its largest and most important, to the new firm.

The youngest of the Scrivener's partners, Tom McDonald, has recently expressed a number of concerns to the others and has suggested that unless a more proactive stance is adopted, it seems likely that the firm will continue to suffer a decline. As evidence of this, he highlighted the loss of clients to the rival firm, the increased number of formal and informal complaints from clients in recent months, and the limited number of specialisms offered by the firm. Recognition of the possible validity of McDonald's argument has led to the partners having agreed to him conducting a detailed review of the firm.

To help with this, he turned to a copy of *Marketing for Law Firms* that had recently arrived on his desk. As he leafed through the book, his ideas began to crystallise. He thought in detail about each of the elements of the firm's marketing mix and began drawing up his results; these are illustrated in figure 13.1.

Looking at the comments that he had jotted down, McDonald's heart sank as he began to recognise the extent to which the firm would have to change if it was to become truly client-centred. He then turned back to the book and flipped through the pages almost at random, stopping only to note down a few of the questions that seemed to spring off the page. Included in these were those in Chapter 1:
- To what extent have the challenges facing law firms been given explicit recognition?
- What specific plans exist to deal with them?
- Has the responsibility for dealing with these challenges been allocated?

The answers, he realised, were 'not at all,' 'none,' and 'no.'

Turning to figure 1.4, he gave the firm a total score of 15, the absolute minimum. In the case of figure 1.6, the results were very similar. And so it went on. Looking at chapter five, he realised that he and his partners were classic examples of boiled frogs, something which was in turn reflected in figure 5.5 and the uncannily accurate description of the first of the four types of firm. Looking at 5.6, he saw how the description of the firm as ostriches applied almost perfectly.

Faced with this, he put the book down and sat back. What we need, he thought, is an action plan, something which will help us to face up to some of the challenges and capitalise upon the opportunities. Fired with enthusiasm, he turned back to the book and began listing some of the activities and tools that would be of help, including:

- a survey of clients so that he and his partners could understand more fully how the firm was perceived (Chapter 4);
- a more detailed SWOT analysis, with attention being paid to the conversion of weaknesses into strengths and threats into opportunities (figure 7.3, figure 7.4 and Chapter 8);
- a programme of internal marketing (Chapter 11);
- the Ansoff matrix (figure 9.4);
- areas of developing client need (figure 9.5 (b)).

Having done this he sat there in the stygian gloom for a few moments and then began scribbling a series of random questions and answers:

- How many new clients have we attracted over the past year?
  Virtually none.
- How satisfied with us are our existing client?
  Probably not very, but they stick with us either because they cannot be bothered to change or because they are not very demanding.
- How much do we know about our competitors?
  Virtually nothing.
- What are we doing about things like Legal Aid Franchising?
  Nothing.
- Why are we attracting so few new clients?
  Because other firms have got a better reputation.

He sat back for a moment and then added a final question:

- And what sort of future have I got here?

As he wrote the words, he knew the answer only too well. The choice, he thought, was straightforward. Either leave now or drag the firm into the final part of the twentieth century. Always one for a challenge, he turned back to the book.

Figure 13.1 Tom McDonald's initial evaluation of the firm's marketing mix

Product

Positive
- A well-established, albeit rather old-fashioned, reputation for sound no-nonsense legal advice
- Long established contacts with local professionals

Negative
- An appointments system that reflects the solicitors' needs and preferences rather than those of the clients
- Accustomed to working on scale fees
- Closed Wednesday afternoons
- Reliance upon resolving disputes using a gentlemanly approach
- Not at all interested in undertaking litigation, especially Legal Aid
- Limited number of specialisms
- Limited ability to provide good financial planning advice
- Little interest in criminal work

Place/physical aspects

Positive
- Nothing obvious

Negative
- Poor location
- Poorly equipped and old-fashioned building
- The area surrounding the firm is beginning to look rather run down
- A down at heel waiting room that features a variety of different types of chair, some out of date (and torn) magazines and an ill-fitting carpet
- Notice board with out of date and peeling notices
- A rather abrupt system for summoning clients
- The majority of the offices are on the first and second floors
- Toilets are on the second floor
- No car parking for clients

Promotion

Positive
- Nothing obvious

Negative
- A very amateurish leaflet outlining the firm's services that has been printed on poor quality paper

Price

McDonald recognised the particular problems of analysing the fee component of law firms but felt that compared with the firm's competitors, they were probably on the high side. Because of this, he made a mental note to find out what fees other firms locally were charging. In the meantime he concentrated instead upon producing a list of questions to which he felt that he needed answers:

- What funds for expansion could we lay our hands on?
- Is our profit level as high as it might be?
- Are we exploiting all possible sources of income?
- Do we send invoices out on time?
- Do we chase payment of these?
- Are we paying creditors on time?
- What is our cash flow like?
- How cost effective are we?
- What costs are associated with each major dimension of the firm?
- In what areas are costs too high?
- What would be the costs and revenues associated with a series of new services?

People

Positive
- Highly committed senior receptionist
- Committed and skilled support staff

Negative
- Poor people management skills on the part of the senior receptionist
- No real commitment to staff training
- Traditional and rather formal patterns of communication
- Too high a rate of turnover amongst the junior reception staff

Process management

Positive
- Nothing obvious

Negative
- Inadequate computerisation
- The appointments system rarely works on time
- A rather abrupt system for summoning clients

Index

Action planning, 90, 91, 119, 122, 123, 159. *See also:* Marketing plans
Advertising, marketing tool, 12, 13
Audit. *See also:* Marketing audit
environmental, 96
organisational, 98
productivity, 99
strategic, 97
systems, 98

Change,
competitive position, 63
economic, 63
legal, 63
managing, 54, 56, 59, 60
political, 63
technological, 68
Client care, 130, 134, 135
action plan, 143
auditing, 136
implementation, 140
improving, 137
planning, 138, 139
setting standards, 137
Client management, 26
Client philosophy, 103
Client satisfaction, 14, 15, 17, 19, 27, 32, 39
Client segmentation, 124, 125

Client service, 30, 36, 109, 113
Client surveys, 42, 44, 45, 46
Clients,
benefits to, 27, 28, 33, 34, 109
feedback from, 40
firm's emphasis on, 27, 30
legal services offered, 29, 109
needs, 33, 115, 116
Communications, 26
Competition,
competitive advantage, 15
competitive position, 14, 15, 19
differentiation, 17
Costs, understanding, 120

Development, new services, 26

Efficiency, 106
Environment,
analysis, 50, 61, 160
changes in, 54, 56
monitoring, 13, 14
social change, 55, 56, 68
structure of, 51

Fee earners, 121

Image building, 13, 14, 16, 117
Internal marketing, 145, 147
action plans, 148
commitment, 147, 149

communication, 148
 implications of, 156
 teams, role of, 150, 151, 152

Leadership, 145, 148, 153, 155, 157
Legal services, types offered, 29, 109, 113

Management characteristics, 4
Management quality, 4, 6
Market research, 39
 client surveys, 42, 44, 45, 46
 discussion groups, 41
 evaluation cards, 42, 43
Marketing. *See also:* Internal marketing
 benefits, 11, 20
 definition, 12, 13, 14, 15
Marketing audit,
 composition, 95
 conduct of, 96
 findings, 101
 marketing effectiveness, 103
Marketing effort, focusing, 123
Marketing information, 105
Marketing mix, 108
 action plan, 122, 123
 evaluation, 169
 product cycle, 112
 product offered, 109
 services offered, 109, 113
 support services, 30, 109, 111
Marketing organisation, 104
Marketing plan,
 development, 77, 80
 implementation, 159
 length, 91
 pitfalls, 92
 strengths, identifying, 81, 82
 structure, 78
 SWOT analysis, 80, 81
 weaknesses, identifying, 81, 82
Marketing process, 20, 22
 analysis, 20, 50, 61
 evaluation, 23
 feedback, 23
 planning, 22, 71, 79, 159
Mission statements, 83, 86

Niche practice, 17

Objectives,
 action plans, 90, 119
 reviewing, 89
 setting, 71, 87, 88, 160

Performance,
 feedback, 14
 monitoring, 26, 142
Planning,
 action plans, 90
 development, 77
 guidelines, 93
 implementation, 159, 162, 163
 objectives, 71, 87, 88
 pitfalls, 92
 planning skills, 73
 process, 72, 79
 purpose, 72
 review meetings, 160
Premises, 26
Price, importance of, 120
Process management, 122
Product cycle, 112
 developing products, 113
 extending products, 113
Product range, 14
Productivity, 95, 99
Promotion, 116, 117, 118, 119

Resources, 95, 99

Selling,
  marketing distinguished, 13
Services. *See:* Legal services, Support services, Client service
Skills,
  employee, 8
  planning, 73
Staff, 8, 121
  commitment, 160
  involvement, 140
  training, 141
Strategic drift, 53
Strategy,
  importance of, 8, 95, 145, 148
Structure,
  importance of, 8, 95
Style,
  management, 8, 74, 148
Support services, 30, 109, 111, 121

Teamwork, 150, 151
  building, 151, 154
  effective, 152
  motivation, 154
Training, 36, 141

Vision,
  importance of, 145, 148
Vision statement, 83, 86